"This wonderful book surveys theories of laughter from classical Greek philosophers to C. S. Lewis, suggesting how they might enhance Middle School pedagogy. Presenting insights from specialists in both psychology and physiology, it speaks to far more than teachers, however. Both communication specialists and admirers of Lewis will find *The Joy of Narnia* extremely rewarding. Best of all, this book practices what it preaches, providing LOL moments in and through its delightful prose. Readers will be repeatedly transported from "ha ha!" to "Aha!" moments: one of the many benefits of laughter provided by the authors."

—**Crystal L. Downing**, PhD, Co-Director of the Marion E. Wade Center, the most comprehensive archive in the world for published and unpublished materials by and about C. S. Lewis and six of his influences (including several people quoted in *The Joy of Narnia*)

"Can a book be both cheerful and thought-provoking? Challenging and approachable? How about funny and yet (at the same time) serious and substantial? *The Joy of Narnia* embodies every one of these qualities and illustrates the many ways that C. S. Lewis's Narnia stories do the same. I admire this book for its breadth of scholarship; I enjoyed it for its play and practicality. I heartily recommend it!"

—**Diana Pavlac Glyer**, PhD, Professor, the Honors College at Azusa Pacific University and author of *Bandersnatch: C. S. Lewis, J. R. R. Tolkien and the Creative Collaboration of the Inklings*

"The tone of Terry Lindvall and his colleagues' *The Joy of Narnia* is light and entertaining, but it is also remarkably insightful. Laughter in Middle School is an important, but mostly neglected, field of study, and this practical book fills this important void. It gives significant insight into serious subjects of pedagogy, but it does so in an entertaining way. Drawing heavily from C. S. Lewis's many books, including *The Lion, the Witch, and the Wardrobe*, the workbook also interrupts with many amusing and insightful examples of the authors' own lives. This is a must-read both for teachers and for students in Middle Schools."

—**Don Nilsen**, PhD, Assistant Dean, Arizona State University Emeritus, Co-Founder of International Society for Humor Studies

"Funny, I think Terry Lindvall, Cary Joseph, and Caroline Joseph might be onto something here! Their new book offers a unique look at the history and impact of humor used in educational settings. As a former teacher, coach, school principal, and university faculty, I can attest to the awesome power of humor in the schoolhouse. Their book navigates the perspectives of the ancient Greek philosophers' views on the role of humor in learning, and introduces us to contemporary educational experts like Parker Palmer, who advocate for humor as a teaching tool. They use C. S. Lewis's *Chronicles of Narnia* as the backdrop to illustrate how humor can greatly enhance the educational experience for Middle and High School students. I think this work should be considered a key curriculum component for any teacher preparation program and simply put, this book is a must-read for teachers, school social workers, and anyone interested in introducing humor into the learning process."

—**Kurt Kreassig**, EdD, Dean of Education, Regent University

"Let teachers know: the more children can let loose and practice the value of laughter, the more equipped they'll be for what lies ahead."

—**Tony Hale**, Actor (Forky in *Toy Story 4*; Fear in *Inside Out 2*)

The Joy of Narnia

Teaching Laughter to
Middle School Students

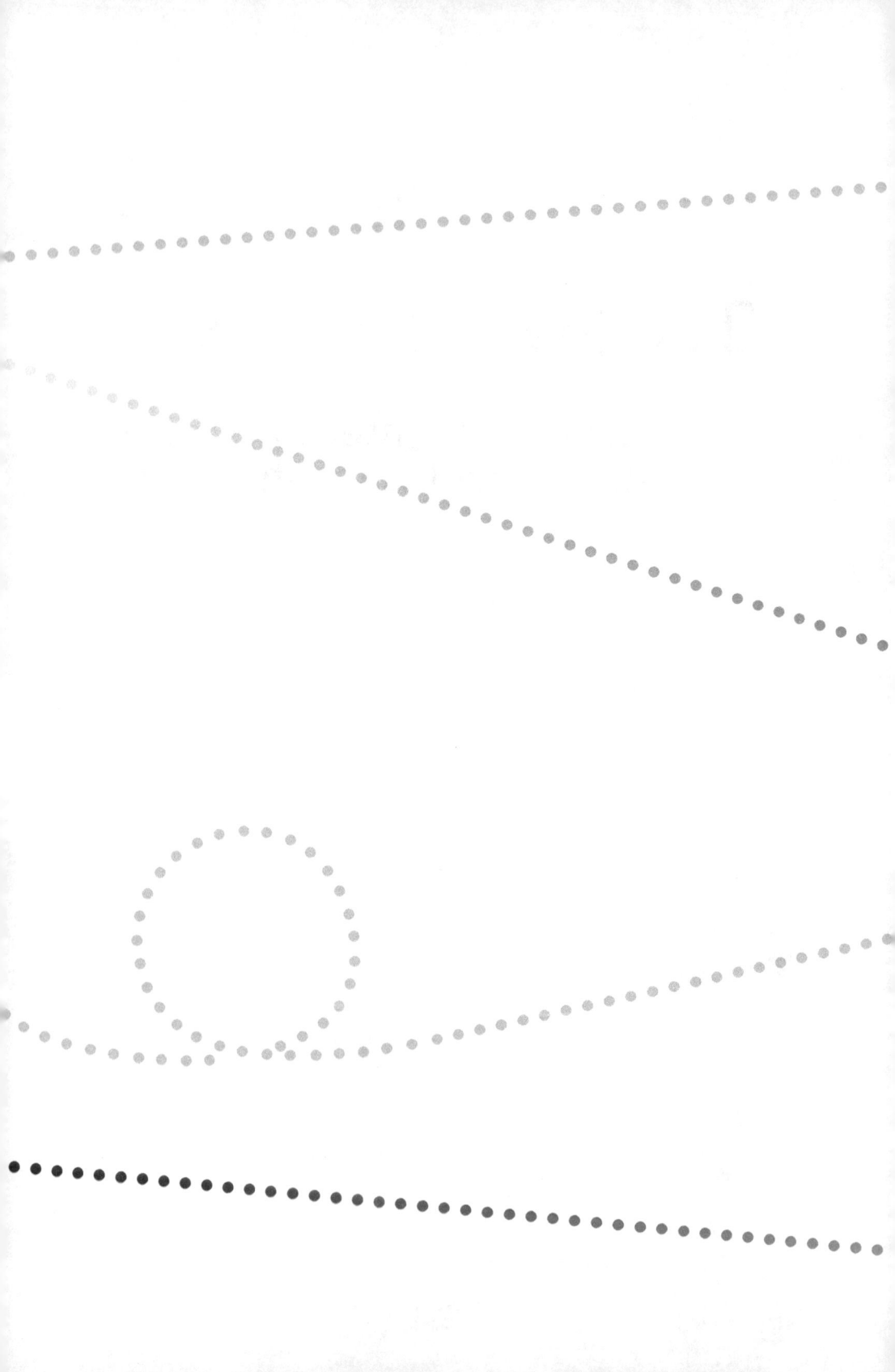

The Joy of Narnia

Teaching Laughter to Middle School Students

TERRY LINDVALL, CARY JOSEPH,
AND CAROLINE JOSEPH

Integratio Press
Pasco, Washington

This is a publication of Foundations, a Division of Integratio Press.

integratiopress.com

Integratio Press is an Imprint of the Christianity and Communication Studies Network.
11503 Easton Dr.
Pasco, WA 99301

www.theccsn.com

Cover design: Carol O'Callaghan
Interior design: Carol O'Callaghan
Cover Image: "Folly Speaks" (Hans Holbein in Erasmus's *In Praise of Folly*, 1509), in public domain

PAPERBACK ISBN: 978-1-959685-21-0
EBOOK ISBN: 978-1-959685-22-7

Library of Congress Control Number: 2024948635

To Joy Joseph

Table of Contents

List of Figures

Acknowledgements

WE, THE THREE AUTHORS, wish to thank key people who jollied us along our journey through lands of woe and lands of laughter. During the writing of this book, a wonderful baby girl was born and too many funny dear friends died. By the grace of God, laughter endured.

First, we thank our persnickety editor and publisher, Robert H. Woods Jr. for his support and guidance.

Second, we thank our families, the Lindvalls (Karen and Chris) (and maybe Molly) and the Josephs (Karen, Chip, Jake, Molly, and Sadie) (yes, two "Karens" in our family).

Third, we express our delight to all our jocund students who laughed with us and laughed at us and to all the teachers and professors who taught us to laugh (mostly at ourselves).

Fourth, thank you to the many fellow Chaucerian pilgrims whose comic stories intersect with ours, we thank Frank and Aimee Batten Jr., Dolly Rasines and Tony Speiser, Debby, Michael and Gloria Rush, and all the laughing saints in Clearfield, Pennsylvania. We offer grins of gratitude for merry colleagues like Craig Wansink, Kathy (Joe) Merlock-Jackson, Bill McConnell and Clair Berube, Ben Fraser, and Reverend Andy Buchanan, and too many others to mention, lest there be several volumes of this book.

For John Lawing and his cartoons (more appear on refrigerators than in his decades drawing for *Christianity Today*), we just send money.

Finally, in Blessed Memoriam 2023, we remember beloved friends of God who made us laugh with unbridled gladness: Kent Rush, George Selig, Barbara Newington, Brian Cochran, Ginni Buchanan, Billy Greer, and Lisa Robertson. May His perpetual Light shine upon each of them.

Introduction

IN 1511, DESIDERIUS ERASMUS OF ROTTERDAM scribbled out *In Praise of Folly*, a lively satire on illiterate and lazy monks, a medieval equivalent of sixteenth century Middle School and High School students. The Dutch polymath wants the Bible accessible for everyone's education and read by the farmer, the tailor, the mason, the prostitute, the pimp, the traveler, and the Turk, but has to deal with some pedagogy matters first.[1] His mouthpiece, Dame Folly, ascends a lectern dressed in motley with a fool's cap and addresses her class, "If you ask me why I appear before you in this strange costume be pleased to lend me your ears, and I'll tell you. But don't bring those ears that you carry to church, but give me the ones you use to attend to jugglers, fools, and buffoons."[2]

Erasmus makes the pedagogical personal. He brings laughter into his classroom to awaken and quicken his students from sloth and stupidity. He does not let teachers escape his wit, warning that if you bring a philosopher to a party (or if you give a mouse a cookie), he will "either sit in gloomy silence or confound the company by turning the occasion into a doctor's oral examination. Ask him to a dance, and you'll get an idea of how a camel waltzes."[3] Erasmus showers the students of folly not only with wisdom, but also with laughter. We hope to bring mirth to bear on learning as we ascend our platform.

History, History, History

Before delving into the substance of this book, we thought it worthwhile to review historical perspectives on laughter and learning. Imagine yourself seated in one of the first classical classes on Laughter and Communication, known then as Rhetoric. You are seated between the tragic poet, Agathon, and the great comic playwright, Aristophanes, with the debauched political figure, Alcibiades, nearby. Socrates lectures on and on about love and the nature of comedy itself, while his hearers become surfeit and sleepy with good and bad wine. You are in Plato's *Symposium*, literally a drinking party, and while he prattles on, Agathon, Aristophanes, and you grow dozy. Plato records that the "others, being drowsy, and not quite following the argument," drop off to sleep, which may have given rise to poet W. H. Auden's aphorism that a philosopher is one who speaks in someone else's sleep.[4]

In his dialogue *Philebus*, Plato's Socrates warns of a dark source of laughter, as a pain in the soul, a vice of malice.[5] Yet one anecdote regarding the Greek gadfly lingers to show his wit. Luca Penni's 1550 painting captures the legend that shows Socrates receiving the liquid contents of a chamber pot from his shrewish, disgruntled wife, Xanthippe, after she had yelled at him. He joked that after the thunder, comes the rain.

The hoary old philosopher who championed the idea of knowing oneself warns that laughter clouds the reason and overrides rational self-control. The guardians or administrators of the Republic need to outlaw clowns and avoid laughter. Laughter, like rhetoric, hangs around the seedy ruins of Athens and gains a bad reputation.

At his own (funnier) symposium, fellow Greek Xenophon writes, "What good men do when having fun is as interesting as their serious activities."[6] The guests not only discuss philosophy, tease each other, drink much alcohol, and make jokes, but they also play Kottabos, a game of skill that involves flinging wine-lees (sediment) at a target in the middle of the room, a sort of spitting contest. At this symposium, the great teacher of Western civilization, Socrates, jests that he is "really good" in the art of matchmaking, perhaps except his own. When Philippos, an untalented jester, fails to get a laugh, he cries, and everyone laughs at him. However, Socrates makes fun of his own advanced age and large belly. More than the professional clown, Socrates makes his companions laugh when he tries to dance. Unabashedly, the classic teacher embodies a pedagogy of laughter. He is no Amelia Bedelia or John Keating (played with panache by Robin Williams in Peter Weir's 1989 *Dead Poets Society*), but he engages his mentees with unbridled playfulness.

Plato's student, Aristotle, aims at rescuing both rhetoric and laughter, conceding in his *Rhetoric* that wit frequently presents itself in the costume of "educated insolence."[7] But like the art of oratory, such mental gymnastics are a valuable part of conversation.[8] In the *Poetics*, Aristotle allows that what is funny is "a defect or ugliness which is not painful or destructive."[9] Comedy is, for this rational Greek, "an imitation of characters of a lower type."[10] For Aristotle, the philosopher of observation and reason, human beings are the only animal with reason, but also the only ones that laugh, or *animal quod ridet*. Yet, even in instructing his student, Alexander, he moderates this gift. A golden mean of laughter teeters between excess and deficiency. In his *Nicomachean Ethics*, he writes:

> Those who carry humor to excess are thought to be vulgar buffoons, striving after humor at all costs, and aiming rather at raising a laugh than at saying what is becoming and at avoiding pain to the object of their fun; while those who can neither make a joke themselves, nor put up with those who do, are thought to be boorish and unpolished.[11]

A Roman in a toga finds his vocation based on Aristotle's Golden Mean, a form of *eutrapelia* (a pleasant and ready-witted "good turn"): standing between the Bore and the Buffoon. The orator

Marcus Cicero brings laughter into the Senate and the classroom, presenting humor as a teachable skill. This urbane Roman Council official and professor of oratory teaches rhetoric and recommends jokes, not "as entertainment, but as weapons of war."[12] He specializes in "brutal put-downs."[13] In his *How to Tell a Joke*, Michael Fontaine selects a series of teachings by Cicero as an ancient guide to the art of humor, where the jest stretches beyond mere entertainment into a tool of rhetorical force. In denouncing his adversary, Cataline, he quips, "no statement is too absurd for some philosophers to make."[14] Accused of being a "laughter addict," Cicero gives us one of the most lucid understandings of incongruity, namely, "The most common kind of joke is that in which we expect one thing and another is said; here our own disappointed expectation makes us laugh."[15] In his *Ars Poetica*, Horace proposes a teaching strategy of *dulce et utile*, educating with delight and profit or usefulness.[16] In particular, he captures why jokes are so effective in teaching, arguing that a joke usually cuts through matters of importance more efficiently and effectively than severity.[17] A wisecrack can expose pomposity and cant. With easygoing generosity toward human frailty and folly, Horace calls for *ridendo dicere verum* ("telling the truth while smiling").[18] Such will be our approach in dealing with Middle and High School students (and University sophomores as well).

A pedagogy of folly subverts the Apollonian environment of the classroom. The late nineteenth century Germanic model of modern education prescribes rationality and objectivity over lived experience. Like the early Greeks, modernity views laughter as foolishness. Laughter, when it erupts, disrupts. To adapt T. S. Eliot's words, it disturbs the universe of the rational mind and the well-ordered classroom. Yet, in its subversive playfulness, it also enhances learning. In 1912, *The Bookman* celebrated British journalist G. K. Chesterton, somewhat mischievously, as one who communicates with hilarity: "There are times when the most effective way to teach a certain truth is by laughing very hard."[19] Chesterton leads us to a pedagogy of the personal, as Parker Palmer emphasized in *The Courage to Teach*: our best teaching comes from the inner landscapes at the core of our identity, for "Teaching, like any truly human activity, emerges from one's inwardness, for better or worse."[20]

A key motive underlying this book is to help our students "know themselves," to discover their comic perspective, and to assist them not only in recognizing the many facets of laughter, but also how they may be agents of their own laughing behaviors. In spite of all their hormonal and social changes, we want them to know they can choose good laughter rather than destructive laughter.

Opening the Door into Narnian Laughter

In his work, *Understanding Humor through Communication*, Professor John Meyer sees wit and humor as primarily modes of personal communication. Asking, "Why be Funny?" he explores how we can understand the moods and attitudes of others, without employing verbal expressions.[21] As a mode of communication, laughter presents itself as a useful and delightful way of teaching.

In this playful excursion of how to introduce laughter into Middle and High School curricula, two young Middle School teachers and an aging University Communication professor walk into history, into a classroom, and finally into a bar. They bring with them the seven-book series of C. S. Lewis's *Chronicles of Narnia* to glean any insights on models of laughter into schoolrooms of preadolescent teenagers. Thus, this book mines Lewis's categorization of the sources of laughter and his incorporation of children's laughter into his Narnian stories. It tries to answer what Lewis, as an amateur ethologist, understood about the laughter of children and how those findings may relate to the liminal Middle and High School experiences, where brooding and sarcasm wax and laughter wanes.

Now why do we begin with C. S. Lewis (other than the fact that the professor wrote his doctoral dissertation at USC on Lewis's theory of communication)? First, Lewis reflects upon how to write for and how to communicate to children. Second, his Chronicles overflow with episodes of a variety of laughing experiences. (Even though Roald Dahl's precocious *Matilda* described C. S. Lewis as a very good writer, she complained that there were "no funny bits in his books.")[22] Third, Lewis does not condescend to children. He meets them straight on, even in sharing a loathing for prunes with a boy at a breakfast table. Fourth, he writes about laughter and sprinkles examples of it throughout his scholarly and popular writings, so much so, that one dull author brazenly dared to write a book on it.[23] Finally, his principal characters in the series are Middle and High School ages (and once they get into High School, they cannot return).

Lewis's stories are the gateway, the wardrobe if you wish, to investigating the larger question of how the teaching of laughter might benefit Middle and High School kids. What do they find funny? How do their senses of humor evolve from their first physical experiences of laughter into these pubescent seasons? How might teachers inculcate a culture of laughter into their lives?

Into the Woods of Research

In their review of humor in educational settings, John Banas and his colleagues acknowledge the negative aspects of laughter such as derision and bullying, but also identify more encouraging fruit. They report that "educational material presented in a humorous manner may be learned and recalled better than the same material presented in a more serious fashion."[24] Laughter facilitates learning. Students learn to perceive and then resolve the incongruity of a humorous instructional message. However, some may miss the joke. One former bright student with autism took a course in film comedy. She wrote to the professor before the class began and confessed that she might not recognize when something was funny. We agreed that every time I touched my nose, I was trying to be funny. She became the vanguard of laughter throughout the course, leading others into mirth. To recruit a confederate student in the class, a comic plant that conspires with the teacher is a boon and a blessing.

Studies on laughter and learning show how humor enables students to cope better, suggest how "Ha Ha" can lead to a Eureka experience of "Aha!", and distinguish between appropriate and inappropriate uses of humor by educators.[25] Pedagogical use of humor contributes both psychological and physiological benefits to learners. As the hospital charts advertise, laughter reduces anxiety, decreases pain and stress, and increases motivation. It does not, however, curtail the flow of diarrhea.

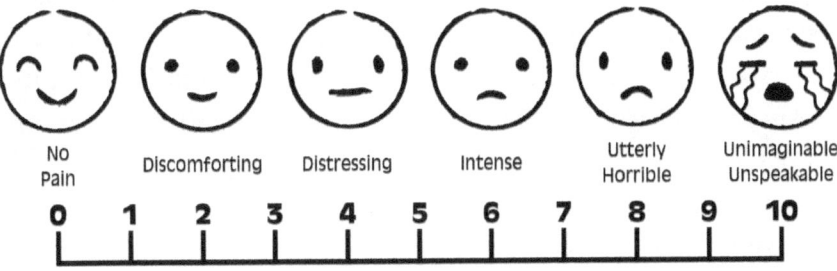

FIG 1. Hospital Charts offer an assessment of pain, according to cartoonist John Lawing. What if teachers offered students an assessment of their happiness before and after a class?

Auburn University professor Bill Buskist notes that everyone knows that teaching is serious (i.e., important) business, but teachers do not have to be serious (i.e., humorless) to be effective.[26] In studying the characteristics of excellent (i.e. master) teachers for the past 20 years, he and his colleagues find that possessing and exhibiting a good sense of humor is an essential characteristic. Humor can also lead to the establishment of student-teacher rapport.[27] He also notes that students report they not only learn a great deal from humorous teachers, but they also enjoy the process of learning from them. Asked for a specific example of teacher behavior that reflects the quality of a sense of humor and promotes student enjoyment of learning, students respond that he or she "tells funny stories or makes witty remarks in class and kids around or jokes with students."[28] Simply, to laugh along with students and use relevant, interesting, and light-hearted personal examples to highlight important points ingratiates the teacher. Recent research also reveals that lacking a sense of humor is a quality that students perceive to be "reflective of poor teaching," and that examples of this quality are "never or seldom telling a funny story or joke, being serious all the time, and not smiling or acting jovially around students."[29] When using humor in the classroom, teachers should ask themselves if humor is helping to improve student behaviors, foster classroom communication, clarify assignments, transition from one topic to another, or enhance the understanding or purpose of any topic or activity. Teachers passing classrooms in the hallway should not be envious of the quiet room, but of the excited classroom where productive laughter can be heard. The use of humor in the classroom is about the development of relationships and classroom atmosphere more than jokes. The most important thing is that students are learning.[30]

The pedagogical use of humor connects it to the use of creativity in learners. Author Arthur Koestler identifies the ability to combine different domains of knowledge as essential to the development of both creativity and humor. Seeing the joke as a form of bait and switch, a student will expect one answer only to be surprised with another. For example, today's lecture will be (pause) given by you. A student experiences the delight of eureka of finding humor in unexpected moments.[31] Philosophers like John Morreall and psychologists like Robert Provine sing in unison that this "pleasant psychological shift" reduces student worries, lessens classroom stress, enhances self-esteem, and increases a sense of community.[32] Provine leads students into becoming ethologists of laughter, following his own scientific approach of observing human behavior under natural conditions and in natural habitats. Through his informal "eavesdropping," students learn to watch when they and their friends laugh. They begin to recognize how men generally seek to provoke laughter (often unsuccessfully) and how women laugh more than men do (usually at men vainly trying to be funny). They see how speakers laugh more often than listeners; how social hierarchy elicits an uneven distribution, with subordinates laughing more frequently than bosses and those of higher status receiving more laughter; and how one can discern the character of persons by what they laugh at. This "sidewalk neuroscience" directs students' curiosity in observing what humans do during episodes of laughing, in class, in the lunchroom, and other settings.[33] It encourages two ways of knowing, as captured by the French verbs, *savoir*, to know about by external observation and experimentation, and *connaitre*, to know from the inside, intimately by examining one's own experiences. These two epistemological acts correspond to what British scholar C. S. Lewis calls "looking at" and "looking along."[34] Cartoonist Gary Larsen drew three primate scholars sitting in front of a mirror and one exclaimed, "For crying out loud, gentlemen! That's us! Someone's installed the one-way mirror in backwards!"[35] When *savoir* and *connaitre* come together, we laugh at ourselves.

Chapter One

C. S. Lewis and Laughter

THE FIRST TIME WE HEAR LAUGHTER in *The Lion, the Witch, and the Wardrobe* occurs on the second page of Oxford don C. S. Lewis's first written Chronicle.[1] In one of his more self-reflexive moments, Lewis describes the four Pevensie children meeting the old, odd-looking Professor with whom they are staying during their evacuation from the London bombings. The second youngest, Edmund, looks at the shaggy old chap and suppresses a laugh, pretending that he was blowing his nose to hide a guffaw. However, caricatures of professors and teachers stand as one of the most comic of all types, mostly because we are rooted in reality. In his science fiction novel, *Out of the Silent Planet*, Lewis confesses to a remarkably sad and funny truth about such educators when his pedestrian protagonist, the bachelor philologist Ransom, explains that a don in the middle of a long vacation is "almost a non-existent creature. College neither knows nor cares where he is and certainly no one else does."[2] Teachers on summer vacation are likewise nobodies, happily for the teachers as well. Even if they see a student out during the summer, they embrace their invisible "nobody" personality and hide as much as they can. (As Nemo means "nobody," the game of finding Nemo takes on new significance for students.)

Four Kinds of Laughter

Our study begins in the eleventh letter of *The Screwtape Letters*. Read deliciously and diabolically on YouTube by Monty Python's John Cleese, the brief missive outlines, however inversely, four main sources of laughter: Joy, Fun or the Play instinct, the Joke Proper, and Flippancy.[3] Our task will be to excavate each of these mainsprings of mirth, exploring not only how they appear in the classroom, but also how to manage each of them.

This work, which may be more of a playful Chestertonian romp than a pedantic lecture, exploits Lewis's models of laughter, as they run amok in a culture of Middle and High School classrooms. Lewis's *Chronicles of Narnia* set forth various categories of what is risible for children. The very sane jester G. K. Chesterton bequeaths to the scholarly Lewis his girth of mirth, a taste of the pineapple, and the *élan vital* of a child.[4] To the Oxford don's grown-up pleasure of beer, he reminds Jack to keep his savoring of lemon squash. Chesterton, observes British humorist Stephen Potter, exhales that "great breath of Falstaffian laughter" that blows away the solemn furniture and hypocritical goodness of the Victorian Age.[5]

With nineteenth century Scottish fairy tale writer George MacDonald and others, Chesterton would not only open the doors to fairyland for Lewis, but also teach him the ethics of Elfland and show its enchantment. Another early twentieth century author of children's literature, J. M. Barrie, echoes Chesterton's delight in fantasy and laughter, with the birth announcement that "when the first baby laughed for the first time, its laugh broke into a thousand pieces, and they all went skipping about, and that was the beginning of fairies."[6]

Tidbit

As MacDonald and Chesterton shaped Lewis, share your comedic heroes as models for your classroom humor. Channel comedians like John Mulaney, Conan O'Brien, Michael Jr., Kevin Hart, or Tina Fey or characters such as Ted Lasso, Ava Coleman, or Barbie to add a zing to lessons that pay homage to the goofs that influenced you.

With the first outburst of laughter in Narnia, we find one of the more common scenarios involving laughter (and one of our favorites) at targeting elderly or eccentric teachers. When the pedagogue dwarf, Trumpkin, instructs young owls on how to behave, the children laughingly imitate him behind his back, all in good-natured fun. One finds an inkling of a comic assignment from this incident. Encourage students to imitate any campus professor's quirks and mannerisms, to parody them in word and image. One relishes seeing enacted caricatures of one's colleagues. All is hilarious until one of us, the short professor, finds a student like Nick, a tall smart aleck, who brazenly enters on his knees, gestures wildly, and speaks quickly—holding up his own professor for comic relief. That student flunks, of course.

Now the names of Sigmund Freud and Henri Bergson appear sporadically throughout Lewis's literature. Both contribute significantly as early twentieth century theorists of wit, humor, and laughter.[7] Although Lewis was familiar with their work, he rarely adopts their terminology when he explores laughter. He is more akin to a lesser-known comic theorist of the early twentieth century who offers some remarkably parallel insights on laughter that corresponded more directly to Lewis's thinking, categories, and language. His name is James Sully.

As one of the founding members of the British Psychological Society, Sully explores the psychology of children and their behaviors. In particular, he probes the nature and development of laughter among children in his 1902 text, *An Essay on Laughter*.[8] While no direct correlation between Lewis's later ideas on the sources of laughter and Sully's studies exist, yet significant overlap pops up in their approaches and conclusions.[9]

Instead of dealing with Freud's tendentious humor sparked by repressed lust or hostility as a window to diagnose unconscious laughter or of looking at Bergson's modernist idea of humans behaving mechanically, Sully opens his work by examining two sources of laughter as joy and play.[10] Thus, he begins with an evolutionary sense of goodness in humans. He writes that certain solemn critics of laughter known as ὁ μισόγελως, (misogelastic) laughter-haters, are so possessed with the spirit of seriousness that the opposite temper of jocosity appears to him to be something shockingly wrong. This estimate of laughter as something unseemly stems in part from the letters of the pompous Lord Chesterfield, in which the writer congratulates himself on the fact that since he has had the full use of his reason nobody has ever heard him laugh.[11]

Lewis's devil named Screwtape begins his eleventh epistle disdaining the laughter of joy and play/fun. The senior devil finds such laughter to be disgusting and a direct insult to the dignity and solemnity of hell. The austere and ravenous devil fits in quite snugly with Sully's laughter-haters. What marks a correlation between the two thinkers, however, is that few other theorists analyzing the comic address the phenomenon of joyous laughter. That Sully and Lewis assert its primacy as the best occasion of *hilaritas* augurs well for a speculative friendship of ideas.[12] For Lewis, one recognizes joy "among friends and lovers reunited on the eve of a holiday . . . Something like it is expressed in much of that detestable art which the humans call

Music."[13] For both Sully and Lewis, this kind of laughter is not simply rooted in an escape from the censors, relief from repressions, or encrusted mechanical behaviors, but in the very nature of the human as a living *incongruity*. As Lewis quips, we are that amazing "oxymoron," a "spiritual animal," an organism that is also a spirit, related on one side to the angels, the transcendent, and the Amish, and on the other side to weasels, skunks, sloths, and academic administrators.[14] Even while diverging on created versus evolutionary origins of laughter, Lewis and Sully agree on many aspects. For example, both accept humiliation and malice, the loss of dignity, and the Hobbesian sudden glory of seeing oneself as superior to others as toxic aspects of much laughter.

For Lewis, these more negative aspects of laughter come after Paradise has been lost, and express themselves in his fallen notion of flippancy, a form of laughter so close to his experience.[15] After many years of teaching, such cynical laughter is a daily temptation.

Sully's primary interest is to tease out the laughter of children, in all its rowdy, roguish, and impish moods. He believes it starts with,

> a sudden rise of pleasurable consciousness, when it possesses the mind and becomes gladness, say the infant's flood of delight at the swinging colored baubles, necessarily dissolves, for the time, the tense, serious attitude into a loose, play-like one.[16]

Sully's insight points to a child's doorway into the fantasy of Narnia when he opines that, "the elemental mood of laughter resembles the play-mood, since it finds its satisfaction in pretense or make-believe."[17] One skips with delight and jumps with jollity in a fresh new world of the imagination. Chesterton notices that while adults may complain of the tedium of a railway station, a small boy finds himself "inside a cavern of wonder and a palace of poetical pleasure. Because to him the red light and the green light on the signal are like a new sun and a new moon."[18]

The Roots of Lewis's Laughter

The phenomena of laughter represented throughout Lewis's fiction provide a conceptual framework for understanding modes, models, and moments of mirth (and malice) in children. Influenced by the comic literature of Edith Nesbitt and Kenneth Grahame, Lewis travels through strange and astonishing lands and then pens his heptalogic series in an attempt to sneak past watchful dragons, the persistent political and religious correctness censors of every age. He writes his ideas indirectly and bathes them in comedy.

Not everyone agrees, however. As we mentioned, Roald Dahl, for example, speaks through his *Matilda*, his precocious 5½-year-old prankster heroine. She read many books and confessed to liking Lewis's *The Lion, the Witch and the Wardrobe*, but that the author has one failing:

> "I think Mr. C. S. Lewis is a very good writer. But he has
>   one failing. There are no funny bits in his books."
> "You are right there," Miss Honey said.
> "There aren't many funny bits in Mr. Tolkien either,"
>   Matilda said.
> "Do you think that all children's books ought to have funny
>   bits in them?" Miss Honey asked.
> "I do," Matilda said. "Children are not so serious as grown-
>   ups and they love to laugh."[19]

Dahl's own mischievous construction of humor for children relies upon comic metaphors and similes that strike young imaginations with hyperbolic incongruities. For example, Dahl sketches a caricature of the abusive Miss Trunchbull, who "always marched like a stormtrooper."[20] In an avuncular aside, he whispers,

> Thank goodness we don't meet many people like her [Miss Trunchbull] in this world . . . If you ever do, you should behave as you would if you met an enraged rhinoceros out

in the bush—climb up the nearest tree and stay there until it has gone away.[21]

Thus, whenever the beastly head appears, children enjoy the horribly funny notion of a large horned animal barging into the room. In a letter to his godchild Sarah, (Lewis wrote back every child who wrote to him), Lewis takes such a preposterous behemoth image and applies it to himself in a much more benign trope. Lewis explains to her how he likes getting his "whole head & shoulders under water in my bath. (I like getting down like a Hippo with only my nostrils out)."[22] His simile is quite similar to the enraged rhino, but much more kindly, benign, and comic.[23]

FIG 2. Former *Christianity Today* Cartoonist John Lawing's rendering of Lewis, the Hippo, in the bath. (Courtesy of John Lawing. Used with permission)

In his study of J. R. R. Tolkien, Tom Shippey identifies about 300 instances of laughter.[24] There are even more in Lewis, but he embeds them in the narratives in normal, unobtrusive ways.[25] They are not slapstick such as bleaching father's hair or gluing his hat to his head, but the jokes, the fun, and even some cruel laughter inhabit the landscape of Narnia as much as enchanted flora, fauna, and food.

Tidbit

In contrast to Dahl, do not stoop to the level of the Middle Schooler of denigrating others. One-upmanship never leads to authentic laughter. Put-downs do not create an environment of respect that encourages students to be vulnerable enough to let themselves laugh. Show students how humor can become cruel, as opposed to cool and encouraging.

Writing for Children

A few critics raise one other concern. As Lewis was a confirmed bachelor most of his life, his friends challenged him for thinking he could write for children. Not only did he have no children of his own, he did not seem to show any particular interest or affection for children. What he did have was the desire to respond to some need of his own to write a fairy tale, or "burst."[26] Three rejoinders should clarify how Lewis came to understand his miniature subjects and to replicate their childish laughter.

First, as we mentioned, certain pieces of children's literature, from Kenneth Grahame's *The Wind in the Willows* to Edith Nesbit's *Five Children and It*, helped to shape Lewis's sense of the comic.[27] The former story gave Lewis a simple and satisfying kind of happiness in the sheer pleasure of the quiddity of things:

food, sleep, exercise, friendship, the face of nature, even (in a sense) religion. That "simple but sustaining meal" of "bacon and broad beans and macaroni pudding" which Rat gave to his friends has, I doubt not, helped down many a real nursery dinner. And in the same way the whole story, paradoxically enough, strengthens our relish for real life. This excursion into the preposterous sends us back with renewed pleasure to the actual.[28]

Such stories, as Tolkien puts it, unveil familiarity, and show a hidden glory. One also learns that food in the classroom may be a cause for celebration, and generously served with dollops of juicy laughter.

More importantly, Lewis, in one sense, stayed a schoolboy, even at the age of 50, when he began to write the Narnia books as "corking good yarns."[29] What he once enjoyed in secret now became a public pleasure. Age gives one a shameless opportunity to speak one's mind, even if it is only yelling, "Get off my lawn, you kids!" His stepson, Douglas Gresham remembers: "In a sense, the child in him lived with him the rest of his life. For anyone who is writing for children, that is an important thing."[30]

Second, as many fantasy book writers, such as Tolkien, Maurice Sendak (in his final interview), and Neil Gaiman, argue, there is no such thing as writing "for children." Lewis championed this idea, particularly in an address in 1952 at the Library Association "On Three Ways of Writing for Children." Railing against bad writing that gives "modern children" what they want, he advocates for better ways to write for them. He explains,

In my own first story, I had described at length what I thought a rather fine high tea given by a hospitable faun to the little girl who was my heroine. A man, who has children of his own, said, "Ah, I see how you got to that. If you want to please grown-up readers you give them sex, so you thought to yourself, 'That won't do for children, what shall I give them instead? I know! The little blighters like plenty of good eating.'" In reality, however, I myself like eating and drinking. I put in what I would have liked to read when I was a child and what I still like reading now that I am in my fifties.[31]

For Lewis (and for great storytellers like George MacDonald and Lewis Carroll), the story "grows out of a story told to a particular child with the living voice and perhaps *ex tempore*."[32] It has a Form that calls to be obeyed and attended to. The actual telling of the story to another human being shapes the imagination and humor of both participants, bringing vivacity and truth to the telling. One must read to grandchildren so that the little tykes can hear you laugh and understand the humor of the world.

Tidbit

David Ezra Stein's Caldecott award-winning *Interrupting Chicken* teaches a creative way to tell stories with quirky humor. Piper, a Little Red Chicken, continually interrupts and improvises on her father's bedtime stories. Once a week, introduce story time in which students can jump in, ask questions, and wildly contribute unexpected and incongruous bits to the narrative.[33] Such an exercise not only teases humor out of students, but it also teaches them how to use their imaginations in creative storytelling.

However, as Lewis did not officially have children to tell his tales to, he practices another way. He explains that writing a children's story was finding the best "art-form for saying something you want to say," for:

just as a composer might write a Dead March not because there was a public funeral in view but because certain musical ideas that had occurred to him went best into that form . . . Where the children's story is simply the right *form* for what the author has to say, then of course readers who want to hear that, will read the story or re-read it, at any age . . . I am almost inclined to set it up as a canon that a children's story which is enjoyed only by children is a bad children's story. The good ones last. A waltz which you can like only when you are waltzing is a bad waltz.[34]

Third, and most cogently, is Lewis's egalitarian belief in the commonality of story and, implicitly, of laughter for all ages. Adulthood should not be seen as a superior state to childhood. Let your inner child out in freshness and spontaneity, in curiosity and delight in simple things. Adulthood is a merely descriptive term, not one of praise. For Lewis, the problem occurred when one was too "concerned about being grown up," for, "to admire the grown up because it is grown up, to blush at the suspicion of being childish; these things are the marks of childhood and adolescence."[35] He adds,

And in childhood and adolescence, they are, in moderation, healthy symptoms. Young things ought to want to grow. But to carry on into middle life or even into early manhood this concern about being adult is a mark of really arrested development: When I was ten I read fairy tales in secret and would have been ashamed if I had been found doing so. Now that I am fifty I read them openly. When I became a man I put away childish things, including the fear of childishness and the desire to be very grown up.[36]

Lewis confesses to a young correspondent that he "[doesn't] think age matters so much as people think. Parts of me are still 12 and I think other parts were already 50 when I was 12."[37] When

William Thackeray scribbles out his Fireside Christmas pantomime for children, *The Rose and the Ring*, back in 1854, he invites his young and old readers to take a holiday, "let us laugh and be as pleasant as we can. And you elder folk—a little joking, and dancing, and fooling will do even you no harm."[38] For Lewis, it would go beyond doing "no harm;" it would add delight, all from a God who is at heart a hedonist. Lewis continues to warn against progress:

> The modern view seems to me to involve a false conception of growth. They accuse us of arrested development because we have not lost a taste we had in childhood. But surely arrested development consists not in refusing to lose old things but in failing to add new things? I now like hock, which I am sure I should not have liked as a child. But I still like lemon-squash. I call this growth or development because I have been enriched: where I formerly had only one pleasure, I now have two. But if I had to lose the taste for lemon-squash before I acquired the taste for hock that would not be growth but simple change. I now enjoy Tolstoy and Jane Austen and Trollope as well as fairy tales and I call that growth: if I had had to lose the fairy tales in order to acquire the novelists, I would not say that I had grown but only that I had changed.[39]

Like the old wedding maxim, Lewis combines something old and something new in his understanding of laughter. He stands both outside and within contemporary research on children's humor. While recognizing the cognitive development of children's humor advanced by Professor P. E. McGhee and others, he also asserts that an adult could hold on to the humorous understanding that children acquire.[40]

Lewis articulates his understanding of laughter, however topsy-turvy, in the diabolical little work that thrust him onto the cover of *Time* magazine in 1942: *The Screwtape Letters*, written a decade before the first Narnian book. As we previously noted, the senior devil Screwtape lectures his inept junior nephew Wormwood on four kinds of laughter: Joy, Fun (or Play), the Joke Proper, and Flippancy.[41] In connection to James Sully's ideas, these categories highlight the unique species that Lewis and Sully seem to recognize: Joy. Various experiences of children match these expressions of laughter throughout the Narnian Chronicles, offering exemplary models of risibility.

In exploring children's humor and giftedness, researcher Doris Bergen emphasizes a "sense of humor" as a characteristic quality of precocious children, of those who recognize the inconsistencies in daily life experiences and dealing with them.[42] For many gifted children, laughter functions not only as a coping strategy, but also as an exercise of true creativity. They develop an ability to appreciate and generate wit and humor, seeing incongruity in various contexts.

Tidbit

While gifted students may show signs of early humor, notice the students who do not laugh and take note. Find a way to check in with these students, and do not be offended if they just do not think you are funny. I once had a student tell me that she did not get my "whole funny-guy thing." I explained to her that I am just trying to share my authentic self with my students. I told her that she does not have to like me, but we do need to find a way to work together. I asked if she would be willing to work with me, and she said she would give it a shot. Throughout the school year, I made sure to check-in with this student to make sure we were both doing our part to work together.

The School Stories of Jack Lewis

Such was C. S. (Jack) Lewis in his school experiences, a gifted child who recognized the incongruities of life, many of which were insufferable. In an autobiography of his early life, he notes how he discovered the cruelty of children while in the British public education system. The chapter in his autobiographical *Surprised by Joy* is entitled "Concentration Camp," just in case we missed his attitude to the system.[43] He detested the kinds of social functions that crammed one's calendar. He resented the schoolboy and schoolgirl dances that he was forced to attend as a messy nuisance. They were a source of torment, not only because he was shy, but also because he felt forced to pretend to be an adult. He writes,

> Add to this the discomfort of one's Eton suit and stiff shirt, the aching feet and burning head, and the mere weariness of being kept up so many hours after one's usual bedtime. Even adults, I fancy, would not find an evening party very endurable without the attraction of sex and the attraction of alcohol; and how a small boy who can neither flirt nor drink should be expected to enjoy prancing about on a polished floor till the small hours of the morning, is beyond my conception.[44]

He also develops a sophisticated vocabulary for so young a boy, which he concedes "must have sounded very funny from the lips of a chubby urchin in an Eton jacket."[45] Lewis is "struck by the curious mixture of justice and injustice in our lives. We are blamed for our real faults but usually not on the right occasions."[46] Of course, any elementary school boy who uses words like insolent and truculent probably needs to be humbled.

Among his peers, he was a misfit. Lewis was useless at games. The sports that other children took to with energy, he fled. He accepted compulsory games as one of the necessary evils of life, comparable to Income Tax or the Dentist. He was uninterested in the gossipy drama of bloods and tarts, and the floggings and canings that would come from the masters. He was also big and clumsy for his age, a great lout of a boy. But worst of all, he confessed, there was his face:

> I am the kind of person who gets told, "And take that look off your face too." Notice, once more, the mingled justice and injustice of our lives. No doubt in conceit or ill temper I have often intended to look insolent or truculent; about on those occasions, people don't appear to notice it. On the other hand, the moments at which I was told to "take that look off" were usually those when I intended to be most abject.[47]

What Lewis will embed in his fiction is this same self-effacing habit of humor, teaching children not to take themselves too solemnly and to laugh at themselves. The pessimistic Puddleglum stands as the exemplary character of such comic self-disparagement, even though accused by the other Marshwiggles of being "too flighty."[48]

Lewis observed, experienced, and reflected upon the vicissitudes of life in comic ways. It was his understanding of himself as a child that enabled him to understand children. For example, he recounts an episode regarding prunes, for which he expressed a certain distaste that gave him an affinity with children. Once in a hotel dining room, Lewis said, rather too loudly as was his wont, "I loathe prunes." "So do I," came an unexpected 6-year-old voice from another table. "Sympathy was instantaneous. Neither of us thought it funny. We both knew that prunes are far too nasty to be funny."[49]

Tidbit

Invite students to share their worst eating experiences or relational experiences (if they are bold enough to do so). Teach them how to take what is miserable in their lives,

what is disgusting, even what is embarrassing, and turn it into a comic perspective. For example, I had a date with a theater major and when we got to the restaurant, she pulled out a puppet and talked with me throughout the whole meal, with other customers looking askance at the awkward interaction. As I found myself talking back to the puppet, I found I was in trouble.

A related issue arises whether the humor of the Pevensie children corresponds to the cognitive development of children's humor from elementary ages through Middle School. Allegedly, Peter is thirteen while Susan is twelve; Edmund is a snarky ten, and Lucy is an innocent eight in *The Lion, The Witch, and the Wardrobe*. These are Elementary through Middle School ages. Remarkably, for an unapologetic bachelor who had no daily connection to children, Lewis captures the developmental humor of children in prescient ways.[50] Lewis lays out his own catalog of the comic, a model of how children laugh and a model for how children might learn of good and bad laughter, imitating the former and eschewing the latter.

A Catalog of Children's Humor

Psychologist Françoise Bariaud investigates age differences in children's humor, noting how a sense of humor develops in the first dozen years.[51] In studying social emotional learning, she points out a key factor of recognizing incongruity with its resolution and practicing "a playful frame of mind," another echo of James Sully.[52] Bariaud emphasizes both cognitively and affectively oriented models of humor development. She stresses how humor in jokes requires an emotional identification with the humorist and a sharing of perceived intent. For example, returning from Narnia and discovering that her brother has visited the white world as well, Lucy looks for a shared celebration of the existence of Narnia with him. She expects the delight of shared play and enjoyment of such a strange discovery of this new land beyond the Wardrobe. However, his lack of an ordinate or proper response leads to a demonstration of a more flippant laughter.

On the question of what a sense of humor may look like in a child, the Development Consultant for Cartoon Network Catherine Lyon differentiates among various options. She classifies the general ability to create or respond to jokes and other overtly funny events or stories. She then explores specific aspects of the talent to tell a joke, the proclivity to use humor to mock or tease in a hostile manner, and the general ability to appreciate comedy.[53] Obviously, it seems, the gift of possessing a sense of humor differs from the ability to be funny, in that the former can recognize the comic possibilities of a situation or a story. A child's sense of humor can taste the comic. A child's wit creates the comedy in the act of invention. The first centers on the ability to perceive and receive; the second to invent and express the comic. The former evolves first in the cognitive development of humor. The child laughs before she makes herself or others laugh. (A key for teaching laughter is that teachers do not need to be funny. They only need to possess a ready sense of humor.)

Tidbit

Take time to recall what cartoon characters make students laugh. (One of us used to laugh at the silent, black and white Felix the Cat going "HA HA!") The Pixar films (such as Ralph Eggleston's 2001 *For the Birds*) depict different kinds of laughter for study. Have them imitate cartoon characters and their silent laughs. (For example, try to laugh slowly like the Sloth in *Zootopia*.)

Lewis seemed to understand the nature of humor among children and his books offer a museum of risible behaviors, of various postures of characters laughing in ways that provide models for his readers. What strikes one in reading his letters to children is how he invites children into a joke, but then nudges them toward creating their own jests. The child reads of laughter and sees it, and possibly imitates it. Lewis calls forth such emulation as an important foundation of teaching when he writes,

> Where the old initiated, the new merely "conditions." The old dealt with its pupils as grown birds deal with young birds when they teach them to fly; the new deals with them more as the poultry-keeper deals with young birds—making them thus or thus for purposes of which the birds know nothing. In a word, the old was a kind of propagation—men transmitting manhood to men: the new is merely propaganda.[54]

We shall soon explore Lewis's four kinds of laughter as evidenced in his Chronicles *and* throughout Middle and High School Purgatory and then try to propagate. As old birds, we will try to teach the younger ones how to laugh, fly, and flourish, imitating us.

Chapter Two

Laughter in Middle School

WRITING OF HUMOR IN THE CLASSROOM, philosopher John Morreall argues that eliciting laughter can "foster analytic, critical, and divergent thinking; catch and hold students' attention, increase retention of learned material, relieve stress, build rapport between teacher and students, build team spirit among classmates, smooth potentially rough interactions, promote risk taking, and get shy and slow students involved in activities."[1] All the positive aspects, physiologically, psychologically, and spiritually, promise a splendid set of possible experiences for Middle and High School students. While school laughter fills the most common category of humorous laughter, occurring "when we are amused by a joke or a funny incident," research draws attention to a functional category of social laughter, used to "integrate the individual within a particular social group," the relevant grouping here being these liminal school years.[2]

Regrettably, laughter in Middle School wanes as teenagers encounter such monsters as bullying, self-consciousness, social embarrassment, identity crises, depression, and other vicissitudes of early adolescent life. Yet it continues to play a crucial role in their social interactions and their emotional well-being. Laughter glues social bonding. Shared humorous perceptions buttress social bonding. When they laugh together, they foster a mutual sense of belonging and bolster a communal security. When nervous, laughter enables them to cope, manage their stress, navigate feelings of anxiety or tension, and even blend into a larger community. A myriad of health benefits exist for those students who do laugh, boosting the immune system and releasing chemical endorphins, dopamine, oxytocin, etc., all reducing stress and enhancing a positive, sanguine mood.

Unfortunately, the weeds of laughter also grow and fester in this fertile soil of laughter. While they develop an increased understanding and appreciation of humor, they also add sarcasm and meanness to a repertoire of comic wordplay (puns, limericks, clerihews), physical horseplay, games, and nonsense. A restless spirit of playfulness resides within them that can burst forth with proper guidance. Otherwise, it might just as easily erupt into a rebellious romp against authority. Peers also shape what they laugh at, with more mature students indoctrinating more naïve ones into sexual, excretory, and hostile humor, the realms of Sigmund Freud's tendentious humor and of François Rabelais's liberating carnival spirit. They will also laugh at jokes others laugh at, even if they do not comprehend them.

Yet this season of life opens up creative insights, with the cognitive development of children discovering ideas and emotions unimagined. Teenagers grasp complex forms of humor and test the limits of inappropriate and taboo humors. One can chart a trajectory of mental and psychological competencies for discerning episodes of comic material, as students fiddle with forbidden forms. They experiment with insult joking, public ridicule, sarcasm, ethnic, racist, and sexist jesting, and sick and dirty jokes, all of which produce laughter, even if, or especially if, they offend authorities.[3]

Tidbit

Develop Habits of Mirth. (Read Arthur Costa and Bena Kallick's *Habits of Mind Across the Curriculum: Practical and Creative Strategies for Teachers* or Stephen Covey's *The 7 Habits of Highly Effective People*).⁴ As one practices laughter (even when one does not feel like it—or especially then), the workout will produce habits of humor and muscles of mirth.

Middle School offers a liminal transition for students. No longer a child and yet not fully mature, these pubescent students grapple with growing up in a season of self-consciousness and hormonal changes. Uncertain how to read the attitudes of their peers, they step warily into this world of change. In particular, they walk gingerly for fear of becoming a laughingstock, of being judged and found wanting, and of being ridiculed. It is easier to withdraw as an introvert than express oneself and be thought a fool. Often the ones who express themselves feel they are met with eye rolls from other students. Increased cognitive awareness stymies spontaneous expressions as they realize how silly they may appear. Teachers can affirm their attempts at mirth, even reminding them that the root of the English word "silly" originally meant innocent and blessed. But that may not be much comfort when you feel they are still laughing at you, blessed or not.

Peer social pressures call them to conform in conventional ways. Perceived social norms dictate behaviors. They may not choose to dare to make jokes, particularly if no one laughs. Or, if they have an unusual laugh, they may censor their own expressions of glee.

Middle School can be a time of intense social pressure, with students feeling the need to fit in and conform to social norms. This pressure can make it difficult for students to express themselves and be their true selves, which can include their sense of humor. Enslaved by self-consciousness, they seek to act cool, which means not showing one's emotions, even positive ones like laughing. Conforming peer pressures, social hierarchies (the inner ring), struggles for attention, acceptance, dominance, or social control, all coupled with a basic insecurity or low self-esteem invite cruel laughter as a means to reinforce social boundaries or humiliate others.

Regrettably, laughter at this stage turns from a communal and affiliative delight to laughing at others. Cliques, such as mean girls, begin to form and one obeys the rules of that coterie. They must assert their conformity by asserting their coolness/hipness/cringeness and becoming flippant.

In certain situations, gifted students find themselves stigmatized because of their intelligence and wit. Facing ridicule or neglect, some gifted students simply isolate themselves; others seek to placate others; and some camouflage themselves to "look like everyone else." However, one of the most positive responses to facing social exclusion in their social environment is to generate a sense of humor. Serkan Demir investigates the ways that gifted students navigate ridicule and handle ostracism in his "I'm not weird; I'm gifted" research; developing the ability to laugh enables them to cope effectively.[5]

The situation requires parents and teachers to create a climate of humor, to enable self-expression, to foster humor, and to model positive modes of laughter.

Tidbit

Offer students an opportunity to answer the question "How are you?" in creative ways. Instead of "okay" or "fine," teach them to use unexpected phrases. I tell them the "boring" words are banned. You cannot just say "good." However, one of us responds: "Old, chubby, and happy," which catches the questioner off guard. Or have them use alliterative adjectives of their first name to introduce themselves.

John Banas investigates, asking "Should teachers be funny?"[6] The general consensus concludes that teachers are not stand-up comics (though some of us try very hard) and are most effective when they encourage humor. However, teachers do not need to be solemn (humorless) to be effective. G. K. Chesterton argued that the opposite of serious is not comic, but trivial. The opposite of comic is tragic or solemn. Thus, education can be both serious and comic, or even trivial and solemn. He continues:

> Seriousness is not a virtue. It would be a heresy, but a much more sensible heresy, to say that seriousness is a vice. It really is a natural trend or lapse into taking one's self gravely, because it is the easiest thing to do. It is much easier to write a good *Times* leading article than a good joke in *Punch*. For solemnity flows out of men naturally; but laughter is a leap. It is easy to be heavy: hard to be light. Satan fell by the force of gravity. He took himself too seriously.[7]

In asking teachers, "Should you be the class comedian?", Drew

Appleby summarizes the extensive research on the *appropriate* use of humor in the classroom, showing many benefits, from an increase in class attendance, learning, and test performance.[8] Material presented with relevant humor is easier to recall. More significantly, one finds that the humor of the teacher encourages divergent thinking; it breaks out of rote learning. It sustains interest in more challenging subjects while creating a positive social learning environment. For many students, when the teacher attracts attention, they sense a reduction of anxiety and stress in dealing with difficult material. Finally, emotionally and socially it enhances a greater rapport among students and faculty.

The Good-Humored Classroom

How might one foster a good-humored culture in the classroom?

First, realize that the educational system conditions many students not to laugh in school. They are afraid of teachers, afraid of peer judgment, and afraid to laugh. Jack Black's character in *School of Rock* looks at his solemn, timid students and yells, "What do they teach in this place?"[9]

In John Banas's "Review of Humor in Educational Settings," nearly 50% of professors use between one and three humorous messages in a class period while 30% use humor four or more times. Of their sample, 20% fail to use any humor at all during class.[10] Interestingly, humor usage decreases slightly in all situations as the semester progresses. In another study, Valerie Downs and colleagues analyze recordings from 40 separate college classes, finding an average of 4.05 humorous messages per 50-minute class. Notably, large differences exist between experienced professors, using 6.50 instances of humor, and inexperienced graduate students, using only 1.60 humorous messages per class.[11]

In a similar study by Jennings Bryant and colleagues, professors incorporate humor an average of 3.34 times per 50-minute class session, or approximately once every 15 minutes. Bryant shows that nearly 50% of professors use between one and three humorous messages; 30% of professors use humor four or more times; and 20% fail to use any humor at all during class. Interestingly, humor usage decreases slightly in both samples as the semester progresses. Analyzed tape recordings from 40 separate college classes show an average of 4.05 humorous messages per 50-minute class. Experienced professors use 6.50 instances of humor and inexperienced graduate students use only 1.60 humorous messages per class.[12]

Tidbit

Start one class with students greeting each other (hands folded and bowing) *only* with laughing sounds. (The Sanskrit term *namaste* means to bend or bow.) Each person approaches another with a slight bend or nod of the head and a fake laugh. As the students mix around the room, the laughter will contagiously become more genuine. Or have students follow the Zimbabwean greeting of clapping their hands when meeting and laughing.

Men generally tell more jokes than women and do so more frequently, but male and female instructors may also be using humor to serve different functions. Dealing with lectures delivered by 70 instructors, Bryant concluded that, "male professors told more jokes and stories, whereas female professors used more spontaneous humor."[13] The study also found that the humor used by female professors was "more relevant to the educational message than those of male professors." Bryant also noted that male professors in their sample used more self-disparaging humor than female professors.[14] We have seen this firsthand in our own classrooms: as a husband-and-wife teacher duo, Cary teaches seventh graders, and Caroline teaches eighth at the same school. Every year, students ask Caroline if she is as funny and interesting as Mr. Joseph. Her response is always, "Nope. But by the end of this year, you'll know the difference between less and fewer." Bryant also reports this fact, that the humor used by female professors is more relevant to the educational message than the humor of male professors.

The Disruptive Class Clown Syndrome

Much of this trained incapacity lay in early elementary teachers' responses to humor.

Lynn Barnett's study follows 278 kindergarten-aged children through their next three school years to determine how teachers, children, and classmates view playfulness. The study assesses perceptions of "the social competence, disruptiveness, and labeling as the class clown," particularly in gender differences.[15]

Teachers report closer relationships with female students, finding "playful" boys to be the most disruptive members of a classroom. By the third grade, teachers view such behaviors as unruly and distracting. Negative views of playful boys paint them as rebellious and labeled as the "class clowns."[16] In contrast, in early elementary years, playful boys and their peers regard the clowning boys as more engaging, popular, and appealing. They are the desired playmates at recess. Few peers see their antics as disruptive, but quite welcome.

In third grade, the persona of the class clown sours the reputations of the playful boys. Barnett points out that the most "startling (and alarming) finding was that the children themselves—most notably the playful boys—who shifted to hold increasingly negative perceptions of themselves as well by third grade. Like their peers, they came to view themselves as unpopular, and less socially skilled, compared to their classmates."[17] They are now problem children. The opinions of the teachers reshape classroom perceptions, even of the playful boys themselves.

The key here is that playful boys incur stigma as unruly and disruptive by the third grade. Teachers prefer more constricting conditions, classrooms that are "rigid," "conforming," and "orderly," with "passive" and "dependent" children.[18] Teachers often condemn behaviors "directed toward themselves or other students, particularly incessant or disruptive talking or chattering, disturbing other students, making unnecessary noise, wandering around without permission, avoiding school work, physical aggression against fellow students, and exhibiting rough or wild behavior."[19] Teachers now symbolically place joking, impulsive, and exuberant "playful boys" in corners wearing dunce caps.

Barnett's remarkable study concludes that educators perceive playful boys as problematic. This attitude, that they are

> disruptive to classroom tenor and have inferior social skills may forebode a longer-term negative trajectory for them as they move through their formal school years. Research has shown that positive student-teacher relationships relate to fewer disruptive behaviors, and when interactions with teachers become increasingly negative, classroom disruptions may become more frequent…
>
> Thus, playful boys who perceive negative affect or criticism by teachers may be at risk. Teachers' perceptions that playful boys have lower social competence, and a lagging rate of social development, may be communicated, and, in turn, impact their peer relationships and acceptance…Thus, teachers' negative assessments of playful boys may pose ominous potential consequences for these children's social and academic development and success.[20]

One can see this tendency emerging in seventh and eighth grade boys firsthand. Playful boys become "problem" boys and join together to cause trouble. Barnett's insights into how educational systems brand playful boys as distracting and disruptive class clowns also augurs the power of a classroom teacher as a Pygmalion, shaping attitudes of play and laughter that excludes them from the classroom and ostracizes their practitioners. Like Plato, they would banish the clown from their classroom Republic.

Turning Lemons into Lemonade

After recognizing the ingrained institutional resistance to laughter, teachers can alter a solemn classroom into a comic environment by their own behaviors. Both affiliative humor and self-effacing humor allay the tension of the early encounters. When the professor appears human, with his own Humor Orientation, laughter ensues. Ed Dunkelblau, former president of the Association for Applied and Therapeutic Humor, consults with "humor-challenged" educators and his primary advice is to laugh at oneself, whenever a mistake or embarrassing moment occurs.[21] If a student answers the question "what ended in 1896?" with "1895," do not penalize the comic. If they are told to name the different quadrilaterals (e.g. rectangle, square, rhombus, etc.), and they scribble in "Bob," "Miranda," and "Isaac," commend them on their linguistic creativity. Or when students start accusing others of stinking up the place, the teacher introduces the game, "Who farted?" and confesses. However, a caveat arises. It is too obvious, but one must be reminded to be yourself. Understand your own peculiar and natural sense of humor. Do not force jokes or stories for the sake of using humor. If you do not enjoy it, do not use it. Professor Stuart Hellman notes that in the three-ring circus of a classroom, "humor used in class should be made fun for both the students and the teacher. If either component, students or teacher, does not appreciate the use of humor, it will not be a positive experience that benefits the classroom."[22]

This leads into doing some research on yourself. Find your HO, your Humor Orientation, as defined by Melanie Booth-Butterfield and her associates in "Funny Students Cope Better." They define Humor Orientation as a communication based personality trait wherein those high in humor orientation have a predisposition to enact humorous messages and perceive themselves as successfully funny across many different situations, often with more inappropriate humor. However, instructors high in humor orientation may be able to use inappropriate humor in the classroom without offending students because they are more skilled or because they are better able to establish a joking friendliness with their students.[23]

For students employed while in college, using humor to cope with stress (i.e., higher humor orientation, HO) associates with "higher ratings of effectiveness, greater self-perceived coping effectiveness, and subsequently with higher job satisfaction."[24] Others perceive supervisors, teachers, and nurses with higher HOs more positively. The study also confirms that Humor Orientation was positively associated with coping efficacy. One might ask, are you a Hi HO or a Low HO or a No HO? Of course, one must be careful in asking this question out loud.

Part of the reason why high humor-oriented individuals may cope better is that they gauge their specific humor enactments to be more productive and effective than low HOs. They feel that they solved the problem, relieved the tension, or generally handled the situation. In addition, the process of encoding the humorous message may focus the individual outward, toward their receivers, and away from their own internal distress.

In Tiffany Freitas's "Students' Perception of Instructor Humor," instructor humor use within the classroom is perceived as an immense benefit to cognitive and affective learning when used correctly. Investigating whether instructor Humor Orientation is a predictor of heightened student intellectual stimulation, interest, and engagement within the instructional setting, she finds that instructor Humor Orientation was the greatest predictor of student interest within the given course, followed by student intellectual stimulation. An instructor's Humor Orientation is also a predictor of student engagement within the classroom.[25]

One sneaky tactic to augment student engagement is to find a helper or confederate (or several) in the classroom, a student you have had before, who can help ignite a comical climate. In one tense moment dealing with phones in the classroom, a teacher plants a fake phone on a student conspirator ready to use it during a class presentation. The teacher grabs the phone and drops it into a pitcher of water on the desk and then throws it on the floor and stomps on it repeatedly. Students are stunned, until the teacher and student confess to their conspiracy to much relief and laughter. However, they communicate the message quite memorably and effectively. Humor provides a humanizing effect on the image of the teacher and allows students to be more relaxed in a secure class environment. Students must feel that they are welcome to participate in creating humor as well. Encourage students to be funny as they naturally look for opportunities to create humor.

Tidbit

Identify class sayings or song ditties. As a means of creating an informal environment, such bits welcome humor and enable students to relax (and then be funny themselves). When psychologist Robert Provine conducts nationwide research into the causes of laughter, he discovers that the most common phrases that accompanied a laughter episode were along the lines of "You've got that right." In fact, it is nearly impossible for someone to laugh and disagree with you at the same

time. The pop-up class repetition of a saying, maxim, or proverb lightens the dullness of a drab day with a humorous reminder of the community.

Chapter Three

On Joy ~
Unexpected Gifts of Delight

FEW WORKS OF LITERATURE EVOKE the rapturous laughter of joy as Psalm 126 (NIV).

> When the Lord restored the fortunes of Zion
> Then were we like those who dream
> Then was our mouth filled with laughter
> And our tongue with shouts of joy.
> Then they said among the nations.
> "The Lord has done great things for them."
> The Lord has done great things for us
> And we are glad indeed.

A Middle School student sitting expectedly on the last day of class before summer holiday finds herself ready to erupt with the joy of laughter. Unbridled paroxysms of liberated laughter overwhelm the student as it did the psalmist. Something has to give in the face of freedom, in the wondrous expectation of floating into an ether of nitrous oxide. What gives is the hilarious burst of laughter at a new beginning.

As an Oxford satirist featured on the cover of *Time* magazine with his academic heresy being "Orthodox Christianity," C. S. Lewis appears as a lecturer renowned for his wit and humor. As we mentioned, in his diabolical set of *Screwtape Letters*, he describes four causes that evoke laughter: Joy, Fun, the Joke Proper, and Flippancy.[1] From these fonts spring fresh and bitter waters that teach Middle and High School students a variety of risible experiences that explain their own behaviors and those of others.

Among Lewis's four categories of laughter, the highest, almost musical, sound gushes from experiences of Joy, an ineffable and sublime experience found in reunions, in victories of the soul, and in moments of grace and love. The foundation of affiliative and blissful laughter grows in the soil of a loving family and community. Its fruit ripens from acceptance and affirmation, which is often lacking for many children; yet teachers can shower it upon children in an uplifting and encouraging school environment. The affirmation of a child can imitate one of the remarkable moments of the Gospels. At the baptism of Jesus, the Father looks down and proclaims, "This is my beloved son in whom I am well pleased" (Matt. 3:17, NASB). The Father accomplishes two major items of affirmation. He expresses His love, and He acknowledges his sheer enjoyment in His Son, and this was before Jesus began teaching, healing, performing miracles, or challenging the lawyers and religious leaders. Take the time to boost students with such positive acclamations and watch as joy washes over their faces.

For Lewis, Joy is "the serious business of heaven."[2] The laughter of the heavens tethers to the presence of Jupiter, clothed with his mantle of the jovial spirit. Lewis scholar Michael Ward illuminates how *The Lion, the Witch and the Wardrobe* conveys the Jovial spirit (of Lewis's favorite planet and favorite mood) in a sophisticated technique he calls *donegality*, a pleasurable quality of atmosphere in Lewis's fantasy that stems from his love and longing for Donegal, Ireland.[3] In his lectures collected in *The Discarded Image*, Lewis points out that King Jupiter brings something out in the character of men, a quality that is "very imperfectly expressed by the word 'jovial.'"[4] In its practice, it is "cheerful, festive, yet temperate, tranquil, magnanimous. When this planet dominates we may expect halcyon days and prosperity."[5] Whenever Jupiter arrives, amazing and glorious things happen. (Planets control each of the books in the series. When Mars marches in *The Voyage of the Dawn Treader*, battles break out in the woods; when Saturn descends in *The Last Battle*, everything looks gloomy; when the Moon dominates in *The Silver Chair*, lunacy runs amok; and so on.)

The sphere of Jupiter, or Jove, is full of "light and music and festal pomp, brimmed with life and radiant in health, jocund and clothed in shining garments."[6] On the Epithalamion of Edmund Spenser, Lewis observes that, "those who have attempted to write poetry will know how very much easier it is to express sorrow than joy. That is what makes the Epithalamion [celebrating a marriage] so matchless. Music often reaches that jocundity; poetry, seldom."[7] Lewis celebrates with all manner of laughter, jollity, merriment, cheerfulness, and blaring trumpets. The devil Screwtape disparages joy as a detestable form of music. Lewis expands on the theme in one of his poems, as Jupiter mounts,

> Where rippled radiance rolls about us
> Moved with music—measureless the waves'
> Joy and jubilee. It is JOVE's orbit,
> Filled and festal, faster turning
> With arc ampler . . . Of wrath ended
> And woes mended, of winter passed
> And guilt forgiven, and good fortune
> Jove is master; and of jocund revel,
> Laughter of ladies.[8]

Jupiter brings jocundity, jollity, and the music of celestial laughter. In Lewis's first Narnia Chronicle, Father Christmas makes an incongruous appearance among the Greek and Norse mythic characters. Yet, as Ward argues convincingly, his laughter and jollity add the right spice to the atmosphere, for "where else can one find a symbol so loud, boisterous, ruddy and jovial who invades and surprises and gives gifts? He is the one most unmistakably born under Jupiter."[9]

FIG 3. On Michael Ward's discovery of Jupiter.
(Courtesy of John Lawing. Used with permission)

Too frequently overlooked is the laughter of children, especially the exhilarating outburst during play, which offers us a pure expression of *joie de vivre*.[10] For children, the most obvious demonstration of the laughter of joy happens in a recognizable experience, reunions. Susan and Lucy experience a happy laughing romp with Aslan after his death and resurrection. The girls fling themselves on his mane and cover him with kisses. Then, after a brief explanation, Aslan with bright eyes and refreshed vigor invites them to a romp. Lucy laughs although she does not know why. Scrambling, leaping, and chasing one another, Aslan catches Lucy and Susan in his velvet paws and tosses them in the air. They stop "unexpectedly so that all three of them rolled over together in a happy laughing heap of fur and arms and legs. It was such a romp as no one has ever had except in Narnia, and whether it was more like playing with a thunderstorm, or playing with a kitten, Lucy could never make up her mind. And the funny thing was that when all three finally gathered together, panting in the sun, the girls no longer felt the least tired or hungry or thirsty."[11]

So too, when all the petrified statues begin to come to life, moving from, what Lewis described elsewhere, *bios* to *zoe*,[12] from routine life to abundant life, the scene is transformed from looking like a museum to a zoo: "And instead of the deadly silence the whole place rang with the sound of happy roarings, brayings, yelpings, barkings, squealings, cooings, neighings, stampings, shouts, hurrahs, songs, *and laughter*" [italics ours].[13] Lucy and her Faun friend hold hands and dance "round and round for joy."[14] Likewise, when the Green Lady of *Perelandra* first sees Ransom, she bursts into laughter, peals of laughter, bending over almost double with her whole body shaking and her hands resting on her knees, still laughing uncontrollably. All her attendant creatures of the planet Venus join in with "merriment afoot: all manner of gamboling, wing-clapping, snorting, and standing on hind legs."[15] Lewis easily captures the playful passion that Middle School students have with their own pets; so much that they load their comic antics on TikTok and let merriment afoot.

Tidbit

Encourage students to stand or sit in the pose of a statue (think of Rodin's The Thinker) or a petrified animal. Then breathe on them (wait a minute—better not breathe on them. Perhaps snap your fingers instead) and have them slowly come to life. If they choose an animal, allow them to communicate laughter as that animal would. A corollary of this exercise is to place a list of animals (e.g. chipmunk, duck, gorilla, pig, crow, seal, rat, woodpecker,

sloth, etc.) in a bag. As a pupil picks a piece of paper, he or she must laugh as if one might imagine it laughing. Other students must try to guess the animal.

A similar experience holds on the other side of death. When King Tirian passes through a stable of death, he looks around him and sees blue sky and grassy country as far as he could see and all his new friends gathered around him, laughing. Joining them all, a great joy overwhelms all the company as they enter the New Narnia, joining the transformation of a New Heaven and Earth. So many happy creatures crowd around Tirian and his friends, all those they believed had died. Their reunion is one of unexpected gladness and joy.

Further up and higher up, all run, race, and gallop and are set tingling all over; the Boar grunts cheerfully. The dogs wag their tails. They look the funniest, as they swim with their mouths and noses full of water spluttering, sneezing, and barking. Poggin shakes hands with everyone and grins all over his honest face. They gather in warm daylight, with "the blue sky above them, flowers at their feet, and laughter in Aslan's eyes."[16] The refrain of "Come further in! Come further up!"[17] sparks communal joy, with a remembrance of all good things. The gathering of all the Narnian fellowship models an idyllic vision of laughter for "there was greeting and kissing and handshaking and old jokes revived, (you've no idea how good an old joke sounds when you take it out again after a rest of five or six hundred years)."[18] His sentiment echoes G. K. Chesterton's wild laughter:

That though the jest be old as night
Still shaketh sun and sphere
An everlasting laughter
Too loud for us to hear.[19]

The laughter of Joy offers a sublime experience, one that cannot be concocted or manipulated into existence. Humans can construct the conditions for other pleasurable forms of laughter, but joy is evasive, elusive, and as whimsical as a breeze. The pleasures of play, of joking, and of flippancy follow Robert Provine's rules of order and construction, but joy is bequeathed like unexpected rain on a desert soul.

Suffering before Joy

Joy often flows out of the crucibles of suffering, separation, sorrow, and woe. That wacky and eccentric Romantic poet William Blake famously pens,

> It is right it should be so,
> Man was made for joy and woe,
> And when this we rightly know,
> Through the world we safely go.
> Joy and woe are woven fine,
> A clothing for the soul divine,
> Under every grief and pine,
> Runs a joy with silken twine.[20]

When teachers communicate that such pain in life exists, students endure it better and cope more realistically. Author Charles Williams told his friend Lewis that when students would often come with their troubles and discontents, "the worst thing we could do was to tell them that they were not as unhappy as they thought. Our reply ought rather to begin, 'But *of course* . . .' For young people usually are unhappy, and the plain truth is often the greatest relief we can give them."[21] Life is quite unbearable if we give them the impression that they should be enjoying its thorns. Lewis suggests that "what is unforgivable if judged as a hotel may be very tolerable as a reformatory."[22]

Weeping at night precedes joy in the morning, as the labors of a woman give birth to celebration. Reunions after a holiday usher in joy, at least until the second bell. The perspective helps. Teachers can help students cope with tragedy and suffering by viewing it as a comma, not a period. Loss, failure, and mistakes are not the end; there is more to the story. When Bart Simpson gets a D- instead of failing, he rejoices with exuberant gladness.

Song and Dance of Joy

Mostly, however, joyous laughter accompanies music and songs. Beethoven incorporated Friedrich Schiller's poem *Ode to Joy* celebrating the freedom and sanctity of human relations (becoming the official anthem of the European Community in 1985 and serving as a protest anthem by Chinese students broadcasting it at Tiananmen Square).[23] For Lewis, music lifted one into transcendent realms, even if in a vaudeville ditty.

As music takes one out of oneself, it illustrates Lewis's definition of humor of offering a "sense of proportion and the power of seeing oneself from the outside."[24] Some of Lewis's jests come directly from all the *Punch* magazines he read as a child as well as from the British music hall tradition, with those vaudeville songs and shticks that the Lewis family enjoyed. Once Lewis and his wife Joy attended a Music Hall Pantomime show where they roared at old jokes and joined a chorus of hearty, raucous singing:

"Am I going to be a bad boy?"
"No, no, no!"
"Am I going to be awful?"
"No, no, no!"
"I promise not to put crumbs in Aunt Fanny's bed
I promise not to pour gravy over Baby's head."[25]

FIG 4. Jack and Joy Lewis enjoy an apocryphal evening at the Old Mo in Drury Lane, London. (Courtesy of John Lawing. Used with permission)

Chesterton contrasts the simple people who tend to sing at their work with the more sophisticated who do not, writing "There were songs for reapers reaping and songs for sailors hauling ropes . . . Why is a modern newspaper never printed by people singing in chorus? If reapers sing while reaping, why should not auditors sing while auditing and bankers while banking?"[26]

Bank clerks, he discovers, are "without songs not because they are poor, but because they are sad."[27] Students, as well, are often without laughter; not because they are dim-witted, but because they are sad. Yet, as Aristotle writes, "Of all living creatures, only man is endowed with laughter."[28] While many may contest such an opinion (especially pet owners), we do know that the potential inhabits deep in those sleepy automatons sitting in our classrooms.

The task of the educator is to educe, literally to draw out, this mirth, even if it means using class singing to do so. Like Donald O'Connor in *Singin' in the Rain*, the call is to make 'em laugh, make 'em laugh, make 'em laugh, through singing (and perhaps falling over).[29]

Tidbit

Sing. Even if you have no voice or tone for singing, put on a recording of a song you want to use throughout the class year. In taking students abroad, they would learn a song from the country they visited. For example, touring Ireland everyone learned to sing Molly Malone:

> **In Dublin's fair city**
> **Where the girls are so pretty**
> **I first set my eyes on sweet Molly Malone,**
> **As she wheeled her wheelbarrow**
> **Through streets broad and narrow,**
> **Crying, "Cockles and mussels, alive, alive, oh!"**
> **Alive, alive, oh**
> **Alive, alive, oh**
> **Crying, "Cockles and mussels, alive, alive, oh!"[30]**

Never had we heard such robust singing with a song no one had heard before. In Middle School, every time students finish a book, we have a "book break up" and play Whitney Houston's "I Will Always Love You." Students

wave farewell to their book in slow motion. They may have hated *Beowulf*, but they enjoy saying goodbye and laugh at the friend they made. Teachers can choose their own favorite song (from Beyoncé to Taylor Swift—the professor doubts if anyone will choose Bob Dylan) to teach and practice.

Dancing in class is more problematic, as one has to move, but it invites a rollicking good time. American *Peanuts* cartoonist, Charles M. Schulz, celebrated Snoopy's iconic dance, one that transports the dancer into a lively ecstasy. Snoopy, "not your average beagle," expresses his ultimate joy in life with his happy dance. He explains that: "To those of us with real understanding, dancing is the only pure art form!"[31] Can one teach students an Irish jig or a square dance? Or perhaps, one can introduce them to the joyous Jewish wedding dance, the Hora. With the holding of hands and the lifting of the bride and groom on chairs (okay, too dangerous and the lawyers will get involved), the movements symbolize the wonders of community and of lifting the loving couple up to the heavens. Such a celebration shows the class that they are not alone, that one dances with others. Even Lewis Carroll asks, "Will you, won't you, will you, won't you, will you join the dance?[32] And if one cannot dance, at least during a break, students can stand and sway like those inflatable tube men you see in car lots.

Tidbit

Become the inflatable tube people for thirty seconds. Or march around the classroom doing the Dialogue Dance. Learn to dance an Irish jig or Hebrew hora. Use online

sources like GoNoodle, NUMBEROCK, and YouTube to your advantage. There are educational and silly dances to most concepts you may be teaching.

Chapter Four

On Fun ~
Unleashed Pleasures of Play

WITH JOY AS THE LAUGHTER OF HEAVEN, C. S. Lewis identifies the laughter of the earth as fun, or Play. What St. Thomas Aquinas (once nicknamed the "dumb ox") calls *eutrapelia*, a good-turning, this laughter refreshes, revives, and almost restores the jollity of Eden.[1] Lewis defines fun as a "sort of emotional froth arising from the play instinct."[2] He finds such divinely given pleasure promoting such virtues as charity, courage, and contentment. For Elementary school, it is akin to an extended, even eternal, recess.

Tidbit

No one has captured the variety and creativity of play as Pieter Bruegel the Elder in his "Children's Games" (*Kinderspiele*) exhibited at the Kunsthistorisches Museum in Vienna.[3] Download an image of the great Flemish painting and challenge students to identify the games they recognize (e.g. leapfrog, blind man's bluff, follow the leader, somersaults, etc.) and to research the ones they have not yet played (e.g. playing the "knot," egg walking,

inflating pigs' bladders, and *morra* (a hand game like rock, paper, scissors)). As a Humanist educator, like Erasmus, he celebrated the human as *homo ludens*; play was not only a vital element of a Humanist education, but salubrious on so many levels, a perspective celebrated by Erasmus: "I'm not sure anything is learned better than what is learned as a game."[4]

Herein Lewis baptizes Greek mythology with delightful abandon, allowing some wildness in the natural gift of Play. When the faun Mr. Tumnus recounts a history of Narnia (including the delights of food with delicious, buttered toast, honey, and sugar-topped cakes), he tells of wonderful midnight dances, milk-white Stag wishes, feasting, and visits of old Silenus on his fat donkey with Bacchus, the wine god. As the streams run with wine instead of water, the whole forest surrenders to jollification for weeks on end. Jollification conjures up partying in its best spirits, liquid as well as communal. It tumbles into a laughter of the earth, with Dryads and Nymphs frolicking alongside trees and flowers. For Lewis, as in Edmund Spenser's *Faerie Queene*, goodness releases energy, vivacity, and fecundity.[5] Evil is repetitive, enervating and boring; goodness is exciting, effervescent, and downright cheerful.

When the spell of the evil Queen of the Green Kirkle (right out of Samuel Taylor Coleridge's *Christabel*) has been broken at the end of *The Silver Chair*, one hears a "hubbub of shouts, screams, cat-calls, laughter, squeals, and bellowings, and fireworks of all sorts rose in the dark air."[6] Little earthmen, with twinkling eyes and merry chuckles, celebrate with unbridled gladness, remembering how to dance a jig and make a joke. The ugly Underworld gnomes, by hundreds and thousands, cheer, leap, turn cartwheels, stand on their heads, play leapfrog, and shoot off huge crackers. They run wildly to the center of the earth. (As a short squirt in a "Junior High School" in 1962, the authorial Professor practiced comedian Jonathan Winters shticks to compensate for a lack of athletic ability. At a new school in Monterey, I performed one Lilliputian comic routine about how thousands of little men escaped the prison of an evil scientist. When an observer saw the riotous behavior, he shouted in panic, "Where are all those little men going?" The scientist cavalierly responded, "After little women you fool!")

The Contagion of Fun Laughter

One of the most obvious empirical findings is that laughter is in need of an echo, that children laugh more in groups than individually. For those who have eyes to see and ears to hear, they say "Of course." The contagion of laughter can spread its own pandemic of play. After Lucy's initial foray into Narnia, Lewis sends his adventurers into worlds of enchantment in groups. They are not solitary Bunyanesque pilgrims, but, almost always, a happy Chaucerian fellowship, who play together and laugh together, sometimes at each other.

Sophie Scott, a rollicking University College London neuroscientist, studies laughter as a social phenomenon, particularly in and through its infectious qualities. Her work delves into exploring how the brain responds to laughter, as it preps a series of facial muscles to join into the human phenomenon. It spreads from person to person just like yawning. Scott points out that, "Contagious laughter demonstrates affection and affiliation. Even being in the presence of people you expect to be funny will prime laughter within you."[7] She suggests how we are wired to mirror one another, to mimic social behaviors in a classroom. When we perceive someone else laughing, we copy laughing behaviors. Psychologist Robert Provine finds that many laughter episodes occur simply because someone else has laughed. Such a communicative cue invites us to catch their socially contagious behavior.[8] (We also learn to imitate such contagious behaviors as coughing, scratching, blinking, and especially yawning.)[9]

Contagious laughter in the classroom, as in larger groups like movie theaters or comedy clubs, also strengthens group cohesion and fellowship. When one finds a group he enjoys and makes him feel good, he looks forward to their company. We relish the gathering of friends who give such positive feelings, even as we recognize our shared laughter offers the molecular building blocks of friendship. Provine extends this observation by noting that, "you're 30 times more likely to laugh with other people than you are on your own . . . the contagious laugh response is immediate and involuntary, involving the most direct communication possible between people: brain to brain."[10] Such research findings derive out of an ongoing investigation to what makes "humans chortle, guffaw, giggle, titter and more."[11]

Eleni Loizou analyzes the connection of children's humorous activities and their play (with materials, with language, as pretend play, and as physical play).[12] Children creatively transform all forms of play into humorous events. Key to the creative invention of the children is social interaction.[13] In play, until selfishness or meanness intrude, children establish bonds through shared laughter. Psychologist William James notes that "we don't laugh because we're happy; we're happy because we laugh."[14] That inaugural laughter has a significant social dimension to it. Rod Martin writes about its bonding effect.[15] Certain individuals possess a gift to laugh and evoke laughter in others. In a study on social laughter, Oxford University professor Robin Dunbar and other scholars look at how laughter sparks social bonding. While a control group sits in a sterile, laughter-free laboratory setting for 30 minutes, other participants watch close friends laughing out-loud as they watch comedy sketches.[16] Those observing laughing friends succumb to shared mirth. Contagious social laughter stimulates endorphin release. The study explains that because social laughter leads to similar chemical responses in the brain, this allows significant expansion of human social networks: laughter is highly contagious, and the endorphin response may thus easily spread through large groups that laugh together.[17] According to Sara Algoe of the University of North Carolina, "shared laughter signals that [people] see the world in the same way. Perceived similarity ends up being an important part of the story of relationships."[18] Contagious laughter not only binds people together, but also enhances the quality of the community.

Tidbit

Sit in groups of three and engage in conversations using only laughter. Share what happened to you yesterday using only giggles, guffaws, titters, and hoots. (The body cannot tell the difference between fake and artificial laughter and that which begins in pretense will become genuine after a minute or so.) No words are to be used, only different kinds of laughter for 60 seconds. This will burst into a zoo of laughing.

One of the most burlesque, knockabout, and infectious episodes of fun occurs in *The Voyage of the Dawn Treader* on the isle of invisible, not very clever, creatures: the Thumpers, Monopods, or Dufflepuds. These unseen creatures are clowns, each with a mushroom-shaped foot that enables them to jump. They think they suffer a curse from a spell that "uglified" them.[19] These characters not only exhibit high spirits, but they also infect others with their blessed silliness. James Sully sees in such buffoonish behaviors something akin to the play of savages, of things remarkably foreign and wonderfully ridiculous. Much can be learned, he argues, from their "art of social entertainment," that without "luxurious salons, without plate and rare wines, without the theater and the concert hall, they manage to obtain a good deal of genuine, unpretentious conviviality."[20] Among such people, "jokes pass freely and the laugh is long if not loud."[21] G. K. Chesterton echoes such behavior, suggesting that, "a man must sacrifice himself to the God of Laughter" and give himself over to laughter just as he gives himself over to God or love.[22] He writes:

> There is no necessary connection between wit and mirth. A man's wit overpowers his enemies; but his mirth overpowers him. As long as a man is merely witty he can be quite dignified; in other words, as long as he is witty he can be entirely solemn. But if he is mirthful he at once abandons dignity, which is another name for solemnity, which is another name for spiritual pride. A mere humorist is merely admirable; but a man laughing is laughable. He spreads the exquisite and desirable disease by which he is himself convulsed. But our recent comedians have distrusted laughter for exactly the same reason that they have distrusted religion or romantic love. A laugh is like a love affair in that it carries a man completely off his feet; a laugh is like a creed or a church in that it asks that a man should trust himself to it. A man must sacrifice himself to the God of Laughter, who has stricken him with a sacred madness. As a woman can make a fool of a man, so a joke makes a fool of a man. And a man must love a joke more than himself, or he will not surrender his pride for it. A man must take what is called a leap in the dark, as he does when he is married or when he dies, or when he is born, or when he does almost anything else that is important.[23]

FIG 5. Lewis's understanding of laughter derives in large part from the comic largess of G. K. Chesterton's topsy-turvy world. (Courtesy of John Lawing, April 1, 1996. Used with permission)

Not able to see the Duffers at first, Lucy asks, "Are they as stupid as all that?"[24] a version of the old Ed McMahon question on the Johnny Carson show, asking, "How stupid are they?" When they actually become visible, she bursts into laughter: "'Oh, the funnies, the funnies,' she chortles and asks the magician, 'Did *you* make them like that?'"[25]

"'Yes, yes, I made the Duffers into Monopods,' said the Magician . . . laughing till the tears ran down his cheeks."[26] They watched as the little one-footed men "got about by jumping, like fleas or frogs."[27] They emitted thumping sounds like Spike Milligan noise effects. The magician says that one of the funny things about the Duffers is that "one minute they talk as if I ran everything and overheard everything as if it were extremely dangerous. The next moment they think they can take me in by tricks that a baby would see through—bless them!"[28] When Lucy seeks to affirm that they are not ugly, but actually look very nice, they cheer, "hear her, hear her . . . true for you, Missie. Very nice we look. You couldn't find a handsomer lot."[29] They said this without any surprise and did not seem to notice that they had changed their minds. One thinks of the Dead Parrot sketch in *Monty Python's Flying Circus*.[30] Jokes join in with fun to multiply the mimicry, repartee, and unbridled laughter.

One even finds a precursor to Monty Python's lunacy in the conversations of these jumping dwarfish creatures: "Nudge, nudge, wink, wink; know what I mean?" kind of repetitive conversation.[31] When the Chief Voice pronounces that they do not know about Queens (referring to Lucy), the scores of others chime in "No more we do, no more we do."[32] When the chief throws out an invisible spear, he announces, "That's a spear, that is."[33] The others parrot him, "That it is, Chief! That it is . . . You couldn't have put it better."[34] One finds such comic banter on the British music hall stage with the literalness of a 1940s sketch comic by Sid Field.[35] When instructed on how to play golf, the golf pro told him to address the ball. Field would deadpan say, "Dear Ball," causing audiences to fall out of their seats with laughter. One also detects parallels with the BBC's radio comedy program, 1950s *Goon Show*, starring Peter Sellers, Spike Milligan, and Harry Secombe, to document the manic absurdity, nonsense, and surreal humor (with a little raspberry blowing) with these invisible vaudevillian creatures.[36]

The speed of the comic conversations and the quickfire delivery of funny lines mouthed by eccentric characters bubbles over with playfulness and good humor. When challenged by Caspian for their cowardice in forcing Lucy to go into the Magician's room and face unknown dangers, they cheerfully affirm: "That's right, that's right! You couldn't have said it better. Eh, you've had some education, you have. Anyone can see that."[37] In addition, they add jokes for children, speaking the obvious, with literal ramifications, "'What I always say is, when a chap's hungry, he likes some victuals', or 'Getting dark now; always does at night', or even 'Ah, you've come over the water. Powerful wet stuff, ain't it?'"[38] Finally, when the Monopods discover how to use their one foot as a canoe, a sort of natural raft, they paddle about and have races. Watching them, the sailors open bottles of wine as prizes for their contests, and then "leaning over the ship's sides," they "laughed till their own sides ached."[39]

Imitating voices and actions of creatures from stories students are reading helps to reinforce plot points and make them laugh. The laughter of fun spills over into joy. Lewis shows how fun, even wild fun, participates as Aslan leads a party of Greek and sundry creatures in waking the laughter of all of Narnia: the dryads of the woods (oak men, holly girls bright with berries, regal beeches, pale, head tossing birch girls) come to life; the river gods loosen their chains (which is a bridge); fettered dogs break their chains; and children who had been crying just a moment before burst out laughing. Lewis introduces Carnival to his faerie land. Even Silenus, the drunken attendant of Bacchus, rides a donkey in celebration. The "old and enormously fat," funny man calls out for wine with robust laughter, "Refreshments! Time for refreshments," and falls off his donkey.[40]

The merry abandonment of children to play promotes most of the natural life-affirming aspects of laughter. As we mentioned, some people carry amusement to excess and become what Aristotle called "vulgar buffoons."[41] However, even more dampening are "those who can neither make a joke themselves nor put up with those who do," whom Aristotle categorizes as "boorish and unpolished."[42] Between buffoons and boors, one finds a happy medium, those who practice humor at the right time, in the right place, and to the right degree. This virtue Aristotle calls *eutrapelia*, ready-wittedness, from the Greek for "turning well."[43]

One of the few early theologians to classify humor as play and see value in the mental side of laughter was St. Thomas Aquinas. He follows the lead of Aristotle in his *Nicomachean Ethics* that "Life includes rest as well as activity, and in this is included leisure and amusement."[44] In Aquinas's category of *eutrapelia*, one finds a good turning, a laughter that refreshes, revives, and almost restores the jollity of Eden, with all its frolicking animals. The instinct to play promotes such virtues as charity, courage, and contentment among the players, leading to what Lewis called a *jollification*.[45] Play offers the most abundant source of laughter in physical and mental exercises.

Fun percolates out of the play instinct as the laughter of the earth, of our bodies. It is laughter of Play in its best sense, namely that of enjoying what one is doing. Here the classroom becomes the playground where even the pedantic Immanuel Kant could speak of joking as "the play of thought," in which laughter stimulates the internal organs.[46] One question that sneaks in is how does one jiggle those organs in the realm of education? How does one invite the laughter of play into a regimented series of wooden desks in a square classroom?

For someone like Chesterton, part of the pleasure of fun is to surrender to the quiddity of the moment. Rain outside might be viewed as buckets of water God has mischievously poured down upon us. Waiting for a teacher to get to his point parallels fishing for salmon. Overcoming boredom offers a knightly challenge as fighting the powers of Lethe, of slogging through fields of sleep-inducing poppies in *The Wizard of Oz*. The repetition of a lesson could be transformed into the chorus of a spontaneously composed song. Chesterton tries to teach us to remember what we enjoyed as children, and not lose that delight. He points to the habit of children to want things again. Whenever you read a child a book, what does she say? "Read it again." Whenever you throw a child into the air, and strain your back, what does the child shout? He claps his hands in glee and shouts: "Do it again!" Chesterton reminds us that this is "because children have such abounding vitality, they want things repeated and unchanged."[47] They are not bored with the same thing. For Chesterton, this is proof that even God exults in monotony. As Chesterton writes, "The sun rises every morning. It might be true that the sun rises regularly because he never gets tired of rising. His routine might be due, not to a lifelessness, but to a rush of life."[48] It is possible that every morning, God claps His hands in glee and says every morning to the sun: "Do it again!" And, unlike many of us, He jumps up and starts the day.

Tidbit

Develop a gamification of curricula. Gamification is a neologism (which is inventing a word like gamification, which is a tautology) that means applying concepts of board games, video games, and role play games into educational curricula. Not only is it a great tool for engaging students, but it also allows students to bring their passions for gaming into the classroom. Teachers may decide to structure lessons as levels, adding power-ups and boss battles for students to show how they have mastered skills and concepts in a way that is enjoyable. For example, students would need to complete a series of tasks to level-up. English students must conquer the comma before sieging the semicolon. Biology students must help cells duplicate their DNA before mitosis (or is it meiosis? We teach English). Social studies students can create comic avatars for use in class discussions about

world events— they could participate as the clown, the cynic, the jester, or even the absent-minded teacher (that is you!).

Teachers Who Play

Unsurprisingly, a study with Dutch teachers finds that teachers' higher involvement in play interaction relates directly to children's higher involvement in play. From observing younger children during free time (indoors and outdoors), Giva Skard and Anita Bundy devised a "Test of Playfulness" (ToP). Working from their definition of playfulness as a "disposition to engage in play," they evaluate four dimensions of children's playfulness levels.[49] First, it observes a child's internal motivation independently of external expectations. They play simply because they want to. Second, it studies the agency or internal control of the child's ability to determine or direct the play action. For the researchers, "Players decide such things as who to play with, what to play, and how and when the play should end. When attempting a new activity, a person may be heard to say, 'I was playing with it to see what would happen.'"[50]

Third, it notes the child's freedom to suspend reality in play: "Players may pretend that they are someone else or that an object is something other than what it really is. They may pretend to do something they are not actually doing."[51] Such freedom releases children (and Middle School students) from inhibitions and fear of failure, as they are creatively "pretending." By suspending reality, they liberate themselves from self-consciousness. A freedom from the constraints of reality may introduce not only creativity and pretense, but also clowning and some mischief. Releasing an eighth-grade class to an elementary playground is an invitation to allow awkward preteens to giddily transport themselves back to childhood. Watching middle schoolers squeeze themselves down a slide meant for second graders can make even the most solemn teacher laugh with delight.

Finally, the Test of Playfulness looks at framing, how a child interprets and communicates social cues. This fourth concept compares "the play frame to a picture frame that separates the wallpaper from the picture. He [the researcher] described play as a frame in which players give cues to others about how they want to be treated. To be a good player, a person must be able to both give and read cues. Of course, the ability to give and read social cues is also a part of many non-play transactions."[52] An enjoyable aspect of the communication of these cues is that "in play, cues are exaggerated and thus easier to learn."[53]

Skard and Bundy's study on how these children engage in social play reveals how they incorporate objects or other people into play, often "in unconventional or variable ways."[54] One must trust the imaginative instincts of the students themselves. For a teacher needing control of a classroom, such a posture portends danger and chaos. Nevertheless, what is most remarkable is how the study demonstrates how teachers' playfulness, spontaneity, and silliness (even goofy facial expressions or funny voices) positively relate to higher levels of children's playfulness, enhancing social, emotional, and cognitive development. An added benefit for flexible and daring teachers shows that this relation can be of a bidirectional nature, and that classroom behavior of the children affects teachers' playfulness! Students can teach teachers to play, *if* the teacher can have a disposition to engage in play. A teacher must dare to play.

Tidbit

Using student choice, invite them to invent or introduce a game that you the teacher must join and play. Let them

be the teachers of laughter and you the student. See how they mock your own behavior with much affection, hopefully with some affection. If not, go back into administration work.

Eunjoo Jung and Bora Jin laid down several stages for developing one's pedagogical playfulness: "First, the teachers need to identify their experience and attitude toward play. Next, they need to be taught to pay attention and understand children's play. When these two skills are attained, they will be able to move to the third stage of training, which includes various playful activities allowing teachers to practice playful behavior."[55] One of the primary ways for teachers to engage in play is with comic facial expressions and different cultural accents. Jung and Jin found that "silly facial expressions play a part in teachers' playful behaviors that help young children cope with stressful transitions."[56] So, Tina Fey and Tony "Forky" Hale would make good teachers.

Similarly, Elizabeth Jones and Gretchen Reynolds suggest that practice and exercises in remembering one's own past play can help teachers stay in touch with the child inside them, which will help them act more playfully.[57] Jeffrey Trawick-Smith and Tracy Dziurgot show that teachers who had better education were more likely to perform good-fit play interactions.[58] Teacher training programs should reconsider how to expand teachers' knowledge about and understanding of play and playfulness and how they might develop their own playfulness—information that is unfortunately lacking in current early-years teacher training.[59]

The Health of Playful Laughter

Researchers document the therapeutic benefits of playful laughter to health with significant evidence. When we laugh, chemical endorphins rush into the bloodstream; they enhance blood flow, stimulate alertness, dull stabs of pain, foster a sense of relaxation, provide cardiovascular benefits like aerobic exercise, increase levels of *immunoglobulin* in the natural immune system, and loosen your bowels. Laughter essentially lights up the brain.

When you laugh, or even when you observe someone laughing, you activate the frontal lobe that helps you understand context, the limbic system that modulates positive emotions, and the motor cortex that controls muscles. While the frontal lobe takes responsibility for self-control and rational decision-making, it also helps regulate emotions and interactions with other people. One decision it helps manage is to help you know what is socially acceptable and what is not. This part of the brain is not particularly mature for Middle School boys.

The frontal lobe also controls high-level thinking and problem solving. It also helps students pay attention. Teachers must learn to wait until the frontal lobe matures as when it is not working, you are not paying attention or making wise decisions.[60] However, it is more likely that the non-dominant (usually right) frontal lobe involving imagination, creativity, curiosity, and artistic/musical ability ripens during this age.

The limbic (border) system supports a variety of functions including emotion of fight and flight as well (right side oversees fear and sadness, while the left side governs happiness—as one might remember in Pete Docter's animated film *Inside Out*.)[61] Curiously, it also captures long-term memory and olfactory recollections (happy smelling). Any kid (and the authors of this book) smelling pizza or fresh chocolate chip cookies will immediately respond with left-side happiness.

During times of stress, fear, or pain, the brain's hypothalamus and pituitary gland produce neurochemicals called endorphins. These pain-killing hormones issue forth during pleasure times as well, during eating, exercise, massage, and laughter. Laughter will distance us from such stressors. In fact, in the endocrine system, three other chemicals or hormones make us happy: serotonin (which stabilizes our moods), dopamine (which rewards us during pleasurable experiences), and oxytocin (the "love" hormone released during sex, childbirth, lactation, and even in talking to one's mother on the phone).

One famous test studies a small group in which half the group watches a 20-minute humorous video, while the other half does not. Both groups then take a memory test, with those who watched the video scoring higher. Notably, both groups also had their saliva tested for the stress hormone cortisol (which contributes to cognitive impairment by raising blood pressure and anxiety). The group who watched the funny video had significantly less cortisol.[62]

Tidbit

Invite students to send you a short video that makes them laugh. Choose which ones will work best in your classroom or have each student introduce her choice and explain why it works on her so effectively. In preparation for tests and assessments, play one of these videos to encourage students to laugh.

Laughing raises your blood pressure and quickens your heart rate at first, while the accompanying release of endorphins reduces stress hormones. Along with the facial muscles that contract as you laugh, your diaphragm, abdomen, respiratory tract, and even your back all get a work out. Your epiglottis half-closes the larynx, making you gasp and increasing the intake of oxygen that stimulates your heart and other organs. When your laughter ends, your blood pressure lowers, and you feel tremendously relaxed.[63]

At UCLA, studies on laughter demonstrated the reduction of pain in children with cancer and at Loma Linda University children with AIDS experienced less suffering. Dr. Lee Berk, professor at Loma Linda University Health (LLUH), spent nearly three decades studying the effects of a good laugh on your brain and body, including hormonal and immune systems. Often his son Ryan Berk would join him in public lectures. With his father, Ryan offered his talents as a well-known chef and a chocolatier to highlight the benefits of humor and chocolate for health. Their most salubrious practical tip on how to become healthier was to laugh and eat high quality, organic chocolate. While the "Happy Faces Hospital Pain Charts" marks one's wellness condition from miserable to ecstatic, it suggests laughter, but it does not mention chocolate. Recently, Dr. Berk's research certified that humor produces positive effects on short-term memory in older adults, which may help readers remember what was in the last paragraph if this one had been funnier. Nevertheless, mirthful laughter offers an aerobic benefit of "internal jogging."[64]

Tidbit

In regard to Hospital Pain Charts, classrooms should have similar charts for check-ins with students. Students can write their name on a sticky note and place their note on the face that they feel that day. Teachers can hide check-ins throughout an assessment to gauge how their students are feeling.

While most evidence supports such medicinal facts about laughter, other popular opinions remain suspect. For example, one of our favorite axioms that children on the average laugh about 200 times a day while adults only laugh 15 times is quite debatable.[65] But humor does increase the body's flow of beneficial compounds, many of them with disease-preventing properties. Delthia Ricks summarizes the benefits: "Laughter is aerobic, providing a workout for the diaphragm and increasing the body's ability to utilize oxygen. Laughter increases immunity to infections by instantly increasing a flood of disease-fighting cells and proteins into the body. Brain wave activity changes when we catch the punch line of a joke."[66] She concludes, as have so many others, that, "Laughter truly may be good medicine."[67] (Of course, it does not help diarrhea.)

One prominent case study centers on a former editor of *The Saturday Review*, Norman Cousins. Cousins found in laughter a fresh, healing force to counteract a degenerative spinal condition. Like the miserable poet in Psalm 31, Cousins's body and mind were still deteriorating, despite huge doses of pain-killing drugs. He had read that negative emotions would affect the body detrimentally. Resentment and envy could trigger harmful biochemical reactions in the body. Fretting would gnaw away at its victims until they began to slump, eaten up from inside by their own worry. Anger could set the jaw in stiff, clenched judgment and depression would press down the spirit until the bones went limp.

Then, Cousins wondered, "What would happen if people practiced positive emotions?"[68] Would there be any therapeutic effect to exercising such robust habits of the heart as love, faith, hope, encouragement, joy, laughter? Were there any benefits to living according to the fruit of the Spirit? It was time, Cousins decided, to test Proverbs 17:22: "A cheerful heart is a good medicine, *but a downcast spirit dries up the bones*" (NRSV; italics mine).

Cousins self-quarantined in a hotel room and watched reel after reel of "Candid Camera" shows and Laurel and Hardy films. He soon found, to his delightful amazement, that God's gift of laughter helped to restore his health. He also found that, in general, the beliefs that people live by and the habits they practice serve to advance either their sickness or their wholeness and health.

Tidbit

Invite students to visit someone in a kindergarten, a retirement home, or a hospital and bring laughter into the room. Or take a child to a retirement home and see how the elderly respond with delight.

In contrast to Cousins, nineteenth century German philosopher Friedrich Nietzsche remained a proud, angry, melancholic, and dyspeptic man with a colossal ego. Adolf Hitler allegedly adopted his spiritual concept of Superman (although theoretically, Nietzsche did prefer a god who would dance and laugh). In the early 1930s, Hitler assumed power and quickly set up special "joke courts" to incarcerate those who attempted to tell jokes about his regime, even hanging a cabaret comic from Berlin. In 1934, the new Nazi Third Reich enacted a "Law Against Treacherous Attacks on the State and Party and for the Protection of the Party Uniform," which made laughing and telling jokes about Hitler and his goose-stepping Storm Troopers a capital offense.[69] Many secular tyrants try to repress, imprison, or kill laughter. Sadly, Nietzsche spent the last years of his life in a lunatic asylum, dying of syphilis, and as Cal Samra put it, "helpless and babbling nonsense—in the care of a group of gentle nuns. In his last years, Nietzsche had a glimpse of God, and also a glimpse of the Devil, who bore a striking resemblance to himself."[70]

One may surmise that the philosophies that men and women live by will lead them to health or sickness. The great existentialist writer

Franz Kafka read many of the books of the great Roman Catholic writer Chesterton and commented how "Chesterton is so gay one is forced to believe that he has actually found God."[71] Chesterton himself observes that the pagan is happier as he approaches the earth; the Christian is happier as she approaches the celestial laughter of the heavens. Such laughter was the first sound that Dante heard as he left Purgatory and ascended with Beatrice into Paradise.[72]

A Brief Anatomy and Physiology of Laughter

The apocryphal Dr. Hagerstaff saw that not only was the body funny, but that also there is a strong correlation between facial expression and emotional states. University of California psychiatrist Paul Ekman's research demonstrates that emotions are connected to bodily behaviors, for "By putting on a face, whether of fear, anger or amusement, a genuine emotional reaction is triggered in your body."[73] You become what you put on your face.

John Morreall summarizes it succinctly: "Our eyebrows and cheeks go up, as the muscles around our eyes tighten. The corners of our mouths curl upward, baring our upper teeth. Our diaphragms move up and down in spasms, expelling air from our lungs and making staccato vocal sounds. If the laughter is intense, it takes over our whole bodies. Our eyes tear. We may wet our pants."[74] We see this even in our two-month-old, Joy, minus the teeth. She may have a bit more pants wetting, too.

As a nonverbal researcher, Ekman explores the correlation between emotions and facial reactions with his FACS, Facial Action Coding System.[75] By coaching students to move facial muscles in a certain way, Ekman shows that bodies react according to the face they put on. He studies seven emotions: fear, anger, disgust, sadness, amusement, surprise, and contempt. He shows that if you put a drop of lemon on the tongue of a baby at only seventy-two hours old, her face would show disgust. If students smile at suffering, they do not feel its depths. If they show boredom, they begin to find their situation tedious. Ekman argues that part of our biological architecture brings a psychophysical parallelism, a connection of face and emotion.

For example, how do you show fear on your face? You raise your eyebrows, pull them together, tighten your low eyebrows, and pull your jaw back. If you pretend to be angry, soon you will experience the seeds of outrage. Slouching in class contributes to a feeling of sloth. However, asking students to sit up straight in class makes them feel more alert, confident, and intelligent.

Tidbit

One can run an experiment to illustrate the correlation between facial configurations and emotional states with students by inviting them to place a pen between their lips to force a frown and then the pen between the teeth to yield a smile. One can feel the movement on a continuum between moods of solemnity and intensity and moods of happiness. In an extension of the experiment, students were presented with a set of four single-panel comics from *The Far Side* and asked to rate their funniness. Consequently, "Those who were frowning, with their pens balanced on their lips, rated the cartoons at 4.3 on average. The ones who were smiling, with their pens between their teeth, rated them at 5.1. What's more, not a single subject in the study noticed that her face had been manipulated. If her frown or smile changed her judgment of the cartoons, she'd been totally unaware."[76]

Such physiological insights confirm what the Hebrew Scriptures observed centuries ago: "*A happy heart makes the face cheerful*" (Prov. 15:13, NIV; italics mine).

This verse can function as a sort of spiritual palindrome, where a cheerful face also helps make a happy heart. What you put on your face is what you will become. (One must first practice palindromes: Mom, Wow, Pot top or Top Pot, civic, level, radar, kayak, deed, rotator, noon, race car, taco cat, deified, solos, sagas, refer, tenet, "Stressed Desserts," "Dennis sinned," "Dennis and Edna sinned," "Step on no pets," "do geese see God?", "Mr. Owl ate my metal worm," "Too bad I hid a boot," "Was it a car or a cat I saw?", "Eva, can I stab bats in a cave?", "No, Mel Gibson is a casino's big lemon," and "Sit on a potato pan Otis." If one finds this too taxing, one can appeal to Aibohphobia, the (unofficial) name for an irrational fear of palindromes.) See? Are you not feeling more cheerful already?

In the anatomy of laughter, we find multiple facial muscles contributing to levels of hilarity. Around the mouth, the depressor anguli oris, the risorius, the levator labii superioris, and most importantly, the zygomaticus major and the zygomaticus minor become the underwear of laughter. They control the smile. Ekman's research builds upon that of the French physician, Guillaume Duchenne, a pioneer in electrophysiology. Curiously, but unethically, he demonstrates the appearance of laughter by electrical muscle stimulation on mental patients.[77] They were wired just enough to make them laugh like lunatics. Nevertheless, Professors Ernest Abel and Michael Kruger tested what they called "smile intensity" and found that professional baseball players with full Duchenne smiles (showing teeth and delight—or just delight if there were no teeth) lived two years longer than those who exhibited only partial smiles or no smiles.[78]

The Zygomatic Experiment

Please let us take you through a series of muscular exercises that will help you expand your physiological laughing potential. See the Appendix for a lesson plan version of this experiment.

As we mentioned, the under garment of laughter is the smile, particularly involving the *Zygomaticus Major*, the muscle that connects the corner of the mouth with the cheekbone (the Zygoma). When stretched, it produces the Polite Smile, the one forced onto one's face when an administrator tells a joke. Ekman argued that not all smiles are the same. He identified 18 varieties including the smile of relief, fake cocktail party smile or after-church nice-sermon smile. It begins with the voluntary muscles, used by people to put on a superficial (and even phony) expression of humor. They smile only with their cheeks and not with their eyes, much like the enigmatic Mona Lisa smile, the quintessential zygomatic smile. As Leo Widrich promises, "Smiling stimulates our brain's reward mechanisms in a way that even chocolate, a well-regarded pleasure-inducer, cannot match."[79] It is only the beginning, but it is a beginning.

The best designation of the good and true smile, pregnant with laughter, is the Duchenne smile, "named after the famous scientist who first separated the 'mouth corners'-only smile" and brought in the eye sockets.[80] The *Orbicularis Oculis* includes that fine sheath of muscle tissue around the eyes, used on the beach on sunny days or in the middle of the night trying to see the alarm clock. This muscle "does not obey the will," but is involuntarily animated by sweet and humorous emotions. The Orbicularis adds a squint that gives us crows' feet, bestows sincerity to our smiles, and splashes the eyes with a twinkle.

Here we also discover *Pupillary Dilation*. In non-verbal studies, your pupils get large when you see something interesting. We are attracted, mostly unconsciously, to dilated pupils. Larger, dilated pupils themselves are compelling, hypnotic, mesmerizing. (When restaurants dim their lights, your pupils get larger, which is why one should take first dates to dimly-lit restaurants, where both members of the couple have growing pupils. One is then attracted to large pupils, which unconsciously suggests interest from the other person. So as dilated pupils magnify, the other person's pupils swell in sweet response, each escalating with the burgeoning eyes, like a Tex Avery cartoon. It becomes love at first sight in a dark restaurant—but then comes the daylight.)

The Orbicularis is one of the most under-developed muscles, so students need to practice squinting and holding it as long as possible. Most students start fatiguing in less than half a minute. Just as your face gets tired at weddings because your muscles are not used to exercising, so practicing the Orbicularis exhausts one, and one begins to laugh.

Next, come the *Frontal and Platysma muscles*. The frontal concerns the forehead and opens the face up. If you are bald, the frontal extends the face 180 degrees backward. It often indicates surprise, with one's eyes alternating squeezing and expanding, squashing and stretching, as animators know.

Platysma opens the face down. The lower lip and neck muscles pull down to show teeth. The mouth opens widely, producing a broad toothy smile. Babies respond merrily to such a grin if they know you. If you do not want anyone to bother you in the library, sit around like this.

Dr. Hagerstaff then observed,

When all these steps have been completed we find that the body can produce a complex set of muscular contractions, a coordinated contraction of diaphragm, intercostal, inter laryngeal muscles all proceeded in microseconds by a slight tightening of the anal sphincter . . . for obvious reasons. You never knew that God built that in, but he had to. If He hadn't, we'd be laughing out both ends.[81]

Physical weariness can come when you laugh so hard, you have to hold your face up, even while controlling your lower extremities. The intercostal muscles move out and up the rib cage as the diaphragm lifts and releases laughter, even as the paroxysms of hilarity shut up any possibility of talking and even suppress normal breathing.

One then turns one's attention to the *vocal* and *abdominal* spheres of laughter. The epiglottis plays a significant function as it half-closes the larynx, like a clarinet, increasing the intake of oxygen as you gasp. Your mouth emits various noises. As you exhale air, repeat, "ha, ha, ha." Then try different vowels. "Hee, hee, hee. Ho, ho, ho. Hu, hu, hu!" Barnyards cannot capture all the onomatopoeia running amok out of the vocal cords.

Place your hands on your tummy, preferably on your own tummy, and push in, expelling air as you contract your stomach. Now one surrenders to the belly laugh. An old Chinese proverb warns that one should beware the man whose belly does not move when he laughs. One must give oneself over to laughter as one gives oneself over to love. In the past, women were trained to cover their mouths with polite titters, but when the boffo laugh, the laugh that kills, falls upon the company, one loses all sense of decorum.

Finally, one arrives at the full *kinesic* and *communal* realms. Bodily movements occur in this stage when you start moving around, rocking back and forth, grabbing yourself, slapping your knees, and even pushing other people. Laughter massages your internal organs. We are not sure what that means, but we like the idea. Even in a theater, you may find strangers laughing so hard they hit you. You lose control of your body, in tears, convulsions, and ultimately exhaustion. Now, with kinesics, you exercise your body. Reach down to the ground, as far as you can go. Grab those pudgy toes and rise back up quickly laughing. (However, some of you may complain that if God had wanted us to exercise and touch our toes, He would have put them up nearer our knees.) As you bend and snap back up, laugh lustily, with full lung strength. Slowly raise your arms over your head, emitting those laughing sounds. Now throw your head back and laugh. Stand in a circle and rush toward each other laughing until you bump into each other and fall down.

To unwind, sway like one of those inflatable tube men, the balloon man and woman, the rubbery air dancers. You may then realize that you have participated in an American version of the Bombay Laughing Club, with some of its hearty exercises. Between 1962 and 1964, an epidemic of laughter broke out among young girls in Uganda and Tanzania that lasted for days with subjects overwhelmed by excessive laughter.[82] A similar case occurred in the Toronto Blessing of 1997, where church people, overcome by the joy of the Spirit of God, laughed ecstatically.[83]

One recognizes, however, that "if there is a quantity of liquid matter in you, all escapes indecorously. For the internal agitation and jouncing is so strong that the sphincters are unable to resist."[84] As you may have experienced, if you laugh while drinking milk, it will spill out of your nose. In 1972 in Denver, Colorado, a professor took his blind date to a party for a spaghetti dinner: He was funny. He was witty. He laughed so completely that a noodle came out his nose. He did not get a second date.

God designed a close relation between our bodies and our moods. Thus, there exists a therapeutic benefit to rejoicing in rehearsing our laughter. As Proverbs 15:13 says, "A joyful heart makes a cheerful face" (NASB). As we have shown, a cheerful face can contribute to a joyful heart.

How might Middle and High School teachers (and even College Professors) inculcate a culture of laughter, of reviving *dulce et utile* in their classrooms?[85] How might we think about laughing with or at authors and understand the kinds of laughter they model? We shall try to answer those questions in our last chapter.

Tidbit

Practice this at home and in the classroom. Again, visit the Appendix for a scripted lesson plan.

Chapter Five

Joke Proper ~ Ingenuity of Wit and Jests

IN A LETTER TO HIS GODDAUGHTER SARAH, C. S. Lewis shares a comic anthropomorphic anecdote. He watches as a young piglet crosses a field with a bundle of hay in its mouth, "and deliberately lay it down at the feet of an old pig. I could hardly believe my eyes. I'm sorry to say the old pig didn't take the slightest notice. Perhaps *it* couldn't believe *its* eyes either."[1] This humorous story could work as well as a jest or a parable about students and professors, but mostly it suggests an astounding parallel among animals and humans. While Lewis believes hamsters to be the most amusing creatures, he thinks that guinea pigs go well with "learning German," that is, if they are not exploding in Uncle Andrew's laboratory.[2]

Various studies theorize the relations between the laughing behaviors of animals and their connection to human expressions of risibility. Recent affective neuroscience research points to the relationship of play and tickling that induce vocalization patterns in rats that "may have more than a passing resemblance to primate human laughter."[3] Researchers posit that "rat vocalizations reflect a type of positive effect that may have evolutionary relations to the joyfulness of human childhood laughter commonly accompanying social play."[4] Philosopher of humor John Morreall points to theorists like Albert Rapp who see all laughter as developing from one primitive behavior, namely "the roar of triumph in an ancient jungle duel," leading to a form of superiority humor.[5] However, as the author of animal stories, Lewis sees incongruity as the basis of rational human laughter, even while seeing other playful laughter as arising from the natural earth.[6]

In his Narnian chronicle, *The Magician's Nephew*, Lewis describes the creation of talking animals. The gift of speech ushers in not only an ethic of justice, but also the possibility of the Joke. When Aslan, the Creator Lion, warns the animals not to go back into the ways of the "dumb beasts," one perky jackdaw adds in a loud voice:

> "No fear!" and everyone else had finished just before he said it so that his words came out quite clear in a dead silence; and perhaps you have found out how awful that can be— say, at a party.
>
> The Jackdaw became so embarrassed that it hid its head under its wing as if it was going to sleep. And all the other animals began making various queer noises which are their way of laughing, and which of course, no one has ever heard in our world.[7]

Lewis makes a comic connection between human and animal (with a wee bit of imagination, one can see the Jackdaw as Jack Lewis, whose blustery way of speaking and an awkwardness at social events may have been self-reflective). When the animals try to repress their laughter, Aslan tells them not to be afraid, but as they are no longer dumb and witless, go ahead and laugh. Merriment ensues and then the Jackdaw asks, "Aslan, Aslan! Have I made the first joke? Will everybody always be told how I made the first joke?"[8] To which, Aslan answers: "No, little friend . . . You have not *made* the first joke; you have only *been* the first joke" (italics in original).[9] Then everyone laughed more than ever, but the jackdaw did not mind and laughed just as loud till the horse shook his head and the Jackdaw lost its balance and fell off. His self-effacing laughter creates a community of affiliative laughter, of everyone just laughing uproariously.

Young readers can observe the laughter of such joking, especially about themselves. They can be the willing butt of the joke and the comic instigator.

Lewis foists the most basic puns on his young correspondents as well. For example, he congratulates one litter of kids on their new redheaded baby sister and says, "I never saw a picture of a [baby] shower before. I had to put up my umbrella to look at it."[10] The playful discourse between Lucy and Mr. Tumnus comes out of the music hall tradition with a misunderstanding that is somewhat akin to an Abbott and Costello routine of "Who's on first?" replaced by are you a daughter of Eve, a girl, a human? Their inability to understand the context or geography of the other's world even leads to the Faun misinterpreting Spare Room as "Spare Oom" of the "bright city of War Drobe."[11] Without full comprehension, he just invites her to tea. The simple language games and misunderstandings also encourage young readers to get the jokes and join in.

Tidbit

Hunt down and collect the best and worst puns students can find. For an extra challenge, see if their pun can relate to the content they are learning.

Early adolescents begin to prefer spontaneous, witty forms of humor to the ready-made jokes and riddles. Off-the-cuff wit marks an important popularity factor in peer groups, especially among boys, who tend to engage in more verbal sparring than girls do.[12] Girls are also more inclined to laugh passively at the humorous antics of boys whom they like.[13] Boys, on the other hand, like girls who laugh at their humor. This reciprocal confirmation helps stimulate budding heterosexual romantic attachments.

Young adolescent boys in particular seem to relish entertainment content that pairs absurdist and irreverent humor with more adult concepts or taboos, especially those jokes dealing with sexuality and "nymphs" or things they really do not understand yet (as if they ever will). We do not recommend teachers delve into such matters but remain vigilant about their existence. Students still "find slapstick and other physical displays of humor entertaining," but adding fresh dollops of irony, sarcasm and cynicism, the adolescents engage in more complex, logical assessments of metacognition and social recognition of irony in context.[14] And they like to laugh at those paper symbols of authority, teachers, and themselves. It is healthy if teachers can join in with them. For example, allow some intrepid students to imitate you, your gestures, your common phrases, and your idiosyncrasies. Or, for the shyer, more introverted ones, let them sketch out caricatures, even as stick (or very round) figures that they can all turn in anonymously.

Similarly, jokes surround the old owls and the teacher Trumpkin in *The Silver Chair*, who without his silver ear trumpet, mishears "the girl's called Jill" as "The girls are all killed."[15]

As Glimfeather the Owl tells about a boy named Eustace, Trumpkin responds irritably,

> "Useless? ... I dare say he is. Is that any reason for bringing
>   to court? Hey?"
> "Not Useless," said the Owl. "EUSTACE."
> "Used to it, is he? I don't know what you are talking about,
>   I'm sure."[16]

It only takes a good supper of Pavender fish, venison, pies, fruit, nuts, and wines to cheer the old curmudgeon up. This jesting of Trumpkin by the young owls is a splendid model for teaching children not to fear, but to enjoy and laugh at their elders, even if a bit circumspectly: "But he's so old now he'd only say, 'You're a mere chick. I remember when you were an egg. Don't come trying to teach *me*, Sire. Crabs and crumpets!'" (emphasis mine).[17]

This owl imitated Trumpkin's voice rather well, and there were sounds of owlish laughter all round. The children began to see that the Narnians all felt about Trumpkin as people feel at school about some crusty teacher, whom everyone is a little afraid of and everyone makes fun of and nobody really dislikes.[18]

Tidbit

Assign students to bring in "Dad jokes" or "Mom jokes" or "Grandparent jokes" or "Guardian jokes." Compare them with their own humor. Have them test these jokes on their own guardians and families at home.

An ironic joke of *The Silver Chair* is that mountain rocks that look like giants are actually giants that look like rocks. They are akin to the Three Stooges, so stupid that when they hammered each other's heads, and howlingly felt the pain of stinging their fingers from swinging the hammer, they would forget and do it all over again a minute later. They are slapstick characters right off the British stage. However, what Lewis achieves here is to open up the mental flexibility of readers, to nudge them to see in fresh, comic ways. In *A Whack on the Side of the Head: How You Can Be More Creative*, consultant Roger von Oech tries to break down conformist thinking in the educational system and jolt his readers into novel ways of seeing, imagining, and thinking.[19] He tells the story of a High School teacher who drew a medium dot on the blackboard and queried students as to what it was. Only one answer was forthcoming: "A chalk dot on the blackboard."[20] Educated to give the right answer, students are shackled by a trained incapacity to not think outside the box. The teacher shares how she performed the same exercise with a kindergarten class. They perceived over 50 answers, from an owl's eye to a squashed bug. So, Lewis builds mountains that look like giants and expands the comic vision of his readers to imagine more than a dot on the landscape.

Punch Lines

Scholar Jared Lobdell connects the dots of Lewis's Narnia to early twentieth century *Punch* magazine images. Lewis admitted that he and his brother Warnie, along with reading *Gulliver's Travels* in an unexpurgated and lavishly illustrated edition, "pored endlessly over an almost complete set of old *Punches* which stood in my father's study. Tenniel gratified my passion for dressed animals."[21] Lobdell suggests that such characters as the gnomes of Bism stem in part from *Punch* caricatures of workers.[22] As Lyle Dorsett and Marjorie Lamp Mead show with their edited collection of Lewis's letters to children, the world of Boxen, with King Bunny as a prisoner and colonists as the war party, and the presence of Prussians, seem to reflect the political cartoons of the humor periodical during the Edwardian era.[23]

Visual comedy in Lewis's caricatures of Professor Kirke, of the dogginess of the Talking Dogs (and its "naughty" British humor with Lewis's sly cryptic jest about "girl dogs"), and of the Monopods ("Dufflepuds") point back as throwbacks to *Punch* magazine. "There is no question," opines Lobdell, "that *Punch* was a huge influence in the Lewis household, and those who have read the collection of one hundred of Albert Lewis's dicta that the Lewis brothers put together in 1922 will have seen how often Albert Lewis's comments

ended with a genuine *Punch*-line" (italics in original).[24] The jumble
of Narnia is characteristic of the comic right out of *Punch*. Numerous images of the great British lion, the royal symbol of England
and possibly an imaginative source for Aslan, appeared in Sir John
Tenniel's illustrations. Tenniel, knighted in 1893 for his artistic illustrations, portrays the authority of imperial Britain through this
iconic image of the maned King of the Beasts, roaring and powerful when aroused. Tenniel's proverbial "Ass in the Lion's Skin" from
Aesop clearly reminds one of *The Last Battle*, and the incongruity of
Shift as the disguised anti-Aslan.[25]

We would argue that not only Aslan, but also some of Lewis's
jests, come directly from all the *Punch* magazines he read as a child,
as well as from the British music hall tradition, with those vaudeville songs and shticks that the Lewis family enjoyed. Hilaire Belloc's
hilarious and hyperbolic parodies of nineteenth century cautionary
tales for children, about "Matilda: Who told Lies, and was Burned
to Death" or "Rebecca: Who Slammed Doors for Fun and Perished
Miserably," linger in Lewis's memory.[26] Like German author Heinrich Hoffman's collection in *Struwwelpeter* ("shock-headed Peter"
or "Shaggy Peter"), the dire consequences of not being an obedient
child comically scandalizes with its morbid ends such as "The Story
of Little Suck-a-Thumb," Conrad, who ignores his mother's warning
and has his thumbs cut off by a roving tailor with giant scissors.[27]

Tidbit

**Bring in several cartoons and have students write punch-
lines for the cartoons. Teachers can provide content-
specific word banks for students to use in an effort to
connect to what students are learning. Teachers can tell
if a student understands the content based on their joke/**

punchline. This is a great formative assessment. Compare
***The New Yorker's* "Cartoon Caption Contest" and have**
students participate. [28]

Arrival of Irony

Children around ten to twelve learn to recognize irony, as they can discern a speaker's belief, intention, and attitude. For students to understand irony, recognizing that what a speaker says is undercut by what they mean, they must also comprehend hyperbole or overstatement. Children must recognize the pretense of the utterance, which points to the incongruity or discrepancy between what a speaker says and what it really means. Researchers point to students' understanding of the discrepancy in which the contrast, heightened by the exaggerated context, not only enhances their self-perception as intelligent, but also triggers laughter.[29]

For example, when alerted to an ironic in-joke in *The Silver Chair*, sophisticated children pick it up with glee. The protagonists stumble into an Autumn Festival of the Gentle Giants of Harfang, where they are to be special guests. Jill, Eustace, and Puddleglum, a Marshwiggle, are oblivious of the fact that they are on the menu until they chance upon a cookbook in the kitchen, with its recipes for Man and for Marshwiggle (a bit too stringy and tough).[30] In the scene, much like the later *Twilight Zone* episode in which the alien's book, *To Serve Man*, turns out to be a cookbook, the three walk blissfully unaware into the trap.[31]

Hearing why they have come, a younger giant stares at them and then releases a great guffaw. The giant King and Queen look at Jill who tells them they have been sent saying, "you'd like to have us for the Autumn Feast." Looking at each other, they nod and "smiled in a way that Jill didn't exactly like."[32]

When Puddleglum pretends to get drunk (and he does get a little tipsy, but plays it up like a vaudeville shtick), his language slurs and he licks his lips. One giant looks at his act of intoxication and roars with laughter, "Why, Froggy, you're a man. See him put it away."[33] "Nothing wrong with me. . . Not a frog. Nothing frog with me. I'm a respectabiggle."[34] Puddleglum believes he has convinced them he is a very funny fellow, whom they think is quite tipsy (it was an act, "well, most of it was," he confesses).[35]

Tidbit

Recognize the power of the inside joke. Inside jokes that are shared with a class create a sense of belonging. At the Middle School level, jokes do not get old for a while. Each time you reference the inside joke, you remind students that they are a valuable part of this community—they are included, they are participants, and the other classes just would not get it. Create one of those "You Had to Be There" or FOMO ("Fear of Missing Out") moments for the class using references to works students read together or funny moments that happen during class. We would give an example of an inside joke, but you would not get it. Ask our students.

As in Gulliver's visit to the Brogdanigans (where Lewis writes an aside, "I know nothing so disagreeable as being kissed by a giantess,"[36] summoning up Swiftian (Jonathan, not Taylor) images of giant moles and hairs on the breast of Gulliver's tormentors), the trio are pampered before they are to be cooked, given some rest, and some gigantic toys. A Nurse who prepares them, utters her "Te-he-he."[37]

Giants about to go hunting are talking and laughing as Jill prattles and giggles and puts on her most attractively childish smile to the Queen, playing up to her with fawning obsequiousness. As she pleads with the Queen to run around the whole castle, the Queen concedes, while "the laughter of all the courtiers nearly drowned her voice."[38] It is an ominous sound.

Mean Girls and Boys

Jokes can take a mean turn around the end of Middle School. The taunting and teasing of peers become a contest of mental agility and comic superiority. Lewis's obnoxious character, Eustace Clarence Scrubbs (who "almost deserved" his name—just as Clive Staples Lewis almost deserved *his* name)[39] would make up clever but mean ditties about his Pevensie cousins:

> Some kids who played games about Narnia
> Got gradually balmier and balmier—[40]

Students will join in laughter when a haughty or deserving victim becomes the target, earning their comeuppance or karma. In the newly created Narnia of *The Magician's Nephew*, the talking creatures rush toward the sadistic Uncle Andrew with "roars, barks, grunts, and various noises of cheerful interest."[41] Uncle Andrew hears nothing but Aslan's roaring and the animals howling. He refuses to understand their language as the children do, for, "the trouble about trying to make yourself stupider than you really are is that you very often succeed."[42] When the Beasts speak, he hears "only barkings, growlings, bayings and howlings. And when they laughed—well, you can imagine."[43]

Trying to figure out what Uncle Andrew is, some think he is a tree. When he faints, one of the Bears says, "An animal wouldn't just roll over like that. We're animals and *we* don't roll over. We stand up. Like this."[44] The bear proceeds to rise onto his hind legs, but in taking a step backward, he trips over a branch and falls flat on his back. The Jackdaw, who had previously been and made the first two jokes of Narnia, proclaims with great excitement: "The Third Joke, the Third Joke, the Third Joke!"[45] All of us know some students who exhibit an unrelenting obsession with jokes, and some of us are such people.

To see a taunting bully get his comeuppance is a delight for children. Through the jokes, children sense a sort of justice in the world that laughter will make right. *Gelatophobes*, those afraid of being laughed at, gently metamorphose into *gelatophiles*, those who enjoy laughter, entering a comic fellowship with others, even if they are all animals. The just desert of a character provides an ethical incongruity, when the proud is humbled, a comic reversal of fortunes. In *The Horse and His Boy*, the young protagonist Shasta has come through a battle in which the villainous Rabadash has tried to invade Narnia. He suddenly hears a sound of "breathless and excited, but obviously cheerful, conversation. And then, suddenly, it all united and swelled into a great roar of laughter."[46] Shasta runs to the sound to see what the joke was. A merry company of Lords stand below an unfortunate Rabadash, unceremoniously suspended from the castle walls:

> His feet, which were about two feet from the ground, were kicking wildly. His chain-shirt was somehow hitched up so that it was horribly tight under the arms and came half way over his face. In fact, he looked just as a man looks if you catch him in the very act of getting into a stiff shirt that is a little too small for him. . . . And there he found himself, like a piece of washing hung up to dry, with everyone laughing at him.[47]

As a proud warrior, he could have endured torture, but he could not bear looking ridiculous. Vainly trying to appear fearsome, he rolls his eyes, stretches his mouth into a horrible, long mirthless grin like a shark, and wags his ears up and down. In an aside, Lewis adds, "Anyone can learn how to do this if they take the trouble."[48]

93

Aslan tells him to forget his pride and his anger and accept the mercy of these good kings. But this merely riles his pride and in his mounting anger, Rabadash discovers, to his supreme horror, that everyone "had begun to laugh," for—

> They couldn't help it. Rabadash had been wagging his ears all the time and as soon as Aslan said, "The hour has struck!" the ears began to change. They grew longer and more pointed and soon were covered with gray hair . . . And his arms grew longer and came down in front of him till his hands were resting on the ground: only they weren't hands, now, they were hoofs. And he was standing on all fours, and his clothes disappeared, and everyone laughed louder and louder (because they couldn't help it) for now what had been Rabadash was simply and unmistakably, a donkey. The terrible thing was that his human speech lasted just a moment longer than his human shape, so that when he realized the change that was coming over him, he screamed out: "Oh, not a Donkey! Mercy If it were even a horse—even a horse—e'en—a—hor—eeh-au, eeh-auh." And the words died away into a donkey's bray.[49]

With mercy, Aslan promises him that he will not always be an Ass, and "At this the Donkey twitches its ears forward—and that also was so funny that everyone laughed all the more. They tried not to, but they tried in vain."[50] G. K. Chesterton once quipped that if a man cannot make a fool of himself, the effort would be superfluous. It is part of the democracy of being human, that each of us is such a moron.

Lewis concludes the story, illustrating how jokes connect with justice, for "The villain's legacy was that he became known as Rabadash the Ridiculous and if anyone did anything stupid in Calormene schools, you were very likely to be called a second Rabadash."[51] The overcoming of evil ushers in a feast on the castle lawn, where wine flowed, tales were told, and jokes were cracked.[52] It unleashes a world of play, but a play that delights *and* instructs. Indirectly, the comic scene promises that the arrogant will fall and warns that students who haughtily lord themselves over others will be humbled. Justice and mercy will kiss together.

The Grand Jest of Gender

The oldest author of this book, overriding his two younger colleagues, argues for the inclusion of one more grand incongruity that speaks to older children. Lewis sees a fundamental incongruity in the doctrine of human creation, of God dividing His image into two genders. Male and female God created us. The source of much adult humor resides in there being these two genders, so divinely alike and so frustratingly different. Anyone who puts books like *Nymphs and Their Ways* on the bachelor Mr. Tumnus's bookshelf winks at the reader. Remember this bachelor don wandered through the country to places like Shapely Bottom.

James Sully calls this reciprocal laughter of men and women, a "mirthful attack or bantering" between the sexes and while he roots the battle of the sexes among the "savages," he concedes it is also a modern phenomenon.[53] Savage laughter has the ring of merriment of the playground and the circus, wild and fun. "Savage life," he observes, "supplies us with clear cases of inter-sexual jocosity besides that of the teasing which, as we have seen, is a two-sided game."[54] And one that is equal. As in many medieval *fabliaux*, the wife exposes male incompetence and twits her husband with her merry wit.. What is key is that "these jocose thrusts at the opposite sex are interesting as illustrating the differentiation" of men and women.[55] Boys and girls will laugh at each other as they try (and perhaps fail) to understand each other.

We do not deny that much sexual humor relies upon *katagelastic* tendencies, the proclivity to laugh *at* others. Many do mock or denigrate the other gender. Such humor grounds itself to see a deficit in gender, practicing a disparaging sexist humor. However, in contrast to this deficit perspective, healthy humor laughs heartily and lovingly at differences. As the French say, *vive la différence.*[56] One might extend that to say, "Rire de la différence!" (or laugh at the differences). Married couples are always laughing at each other, that is, until they have a baby. (Now the two younger authors laugh at their baby, Joy). Making jokes on differences, in gender or race or class, bathed in love, becomes not only acceptable, but also desirable intercourse.[57] When Edmund complains about girls for not being able to carry a map in their head, Lucy snaps back "That's because our heads have something inside them."[58] Loving laughter with gender and race is a dance of equals, with undulating movement back and forth.

Tidbit

Based on the works of Hilda Taba, have students write on sticky notes what they find funny and put it on a piece of paper.[59] With small groups, have students make categories and group the sticky notes where they find commonalities. Have them name the groups and see what generalizations they can make about each other's senses of humor. What do they see funny about each other?

This reciprocal laughter of gender differences occurs most brilliantly near the end of *The Voyage of the Dawn Treader*. Taken with the beauty of Ramandu's star daughter, Caspian seeks to break a spell under which three Sleepers sleep. He tells her the story of Sleeping Beauty from his British friends, "a story of a prince coming to a castle where all the people lay in an enchanted sleep. In that story, he could not dissolve the enchantment until he had kissed the princess."[60]

"But here," the girl tells him with quick wit, "it is different. Here he cannot kiss the princess till he has dissolved the enchantment."[61] Eagerly, Caspian asks that he be shown how to accomplish that work *at once*. He sets out on his quest and hopes to speak to her very, very soon, once he breaks the enchantment. And she looks at him and smiles. It is the beginning of a lovely bit of play.

As we mentioned, the "Joke Proper" functions on the principle of incongruity, of comic difference, such as between men and women, or any pairing. As Chesterton observed, we laugh at three things: jokes about bodily humiliation, jokes about things foreign, and jokes about bad cheese.[62] We laugh at *different perspectives*. A former student from Kenya, Enoch, once blew his nose by closing off one nostril and discharging the contents onto the ground. I laughed at him, but he responded with even more laughter, saying "Oh yes, and you Americans blow your noses into a cloth and then place it in your pocket. What kind of person would want to save that kind of mucus?"

Nevertheless, one must attend to the negative aspects of the Joke. In his delineation of Relief theory, Sigmund Freud digs up fallow ground in the relation of jokes to the unconscious. Six years after publishing his classic *Interpretation of Dreams* in 1899, Freud wrote *Der Witz und seine Beziehung zum Unbewussten* (*Jokes and Their Relation to the Unconscious*, 1905) (which is much funnier in German when you are trying to play Scrabble), pointing out similarities between dreams and jokes.[63] He argues that both dreams and jokes use the same techniques to disguise meanings and mask motives through representation, condensation, and displacement, and both require cognitive analysis to interpret their latent meanings. Freud asserts that, "jokes, like dreams and slips of the tongue, bear the traces of repressed desires."[64] Freud was generally pessimistic about humankind, believing that at the root of all experience are neuroses, caused by anxiety. Humans are in a constant struggle to deal with this problem, expending enormous amounts of psychic energy. Laughter functions as a primary vehicle to help us avoid such a mental workout.

Freud begins with the topic of jokes, which he defined as funny anecdotes designed to make another person laugh and are constructed (just like dreams) to help us circumvent one or another form of censorship or prohibition.[65] And, of course, the inhibitions we want to escape are usually sexual or aggressive, or what Freud would call *tendentious*. (One of us suspects that moderns are more likely to repress a moral law than a sexual instinct.) Every joke is thus a victory over inhibition and taboos, allowing us to escape the censors of our rational mind and society.

Jokes allow us to attack our enemy, express our hostile aggressiveness, so that we "evade restrictions and open sources of pleasure that have become inaccessible."[66] Tendentious jokes serve a darker purpose and enable us to show aggression toward those in exalted positions (the great, the dignified, the mighty, and lawyers) who claim authority and who are usually protected by both internal inhibitions and external circumstances, our laughter becoming "a rebellion against that authority and liberation from its pressure."[67] For Freud, there are only two purposes of tendentious jokes: either a hostile joke (serving the purpose of aggressiveness, satire, or defiance) or an obscene one (servicing the purpose of exposure).

For Freud, laughter is rooted in hostility and sexual repression and general dirtiness of the human condition. Rather than a theory of the comic as difference, he marks it as deficit, of a lack, an envy. While elements of truth exist in his theories, little of his comedy resides in the neighborhood of the good or the beautiful. Thomas Hobbes, too, quarantines laughter to the cruel garbage heaps of culture—of course, in Hobbes's world, all humanity is aggressively hostile and competitive. His description of the life of man in his *Leviathan* as "solitary, poor, nasty, brutish, and short" is not one to inspire sanguine optimism.[68]

Critics such as Noel Carroll and John Morreall question Freud's idea of energy management (making a logical connection between expressing pent-up energy versus repressing it).[69] They point out, rightly in my opinion, that in Freud's world, the most repressed and inhibited people would laugh the loudest. Experience suggests that these people do not really enjoy joking. Such a theory also assumes that as psychic energy finds a release in the physical action of laughter, any laughter will be explained by an excess of nervous energy.

Tidbit

Yet much humor can be explained by this theory of relief. Ask students when they have laughed out of embarrassment or stress and whether it helped or not.

In contrast, the observation that many of the jokes we make are vulgar suggested to Lewis that a basic incongruity exists in human nature. The fact that people make so-called coarse jokes (and Middle School adolescents do make naughty jokes) was, for Lewis, ontological evidence of the truth of the Christian doctrine of the fall. He writes,

> The coarse joke proclaims that we have here an animal which finds its own animality either objectionable or funny. Unless there had been a quarrel between the spirit and the organism, I do not see how this could be. It is the very mark of the two not being "at home" together. But it is very difficult to imagine such a state of affairs as original—to suppose a creature which from the very first was half shocked and half tickled to death at the mere fact of being the creature

it is. I do not perceive that dogs see anything funny about being dogs. I suspect that angels see nothing funny about being angels.[70]

In *The Screwtape Letters*, Lewis emphasizes that the Joke Proper turns on a "sudden perception of incongruity."[71] Like these same adolescents, Lewis finds in the fact that we have bodies to be "the oldest joke there is. There's no living with it till we recognize that one of its functions in our lives is to play the part of the buffoon. Until some theory has sophisticated them, every man, woman and child in the world knows this."[72] Discussing sexual and bawdy humor, Lewis divides human responses into two categories. For some, there is "no passion as serious as lust," and they treat indecent jokes about sex as invitations to lasciviousness.[73] However, others laugh at jokes about sex because they give rise to many incongruities. Humor, rather than sexual desire, dominates. Most male writers, from Ovid to Chaucer to Dave Barry and Dave Chappelle, find the opposite gender funny; even as women find men ridiculous. What makes the opposite gender funny is intimately connected to what makes them worthy of being worshiped. The history of comedy between the two sexes favors one side and then the other.

Once, under medication for pain, Lewis suffered strange dreams. One in particular focused upon Purgatory and illustrated his comic perception of the male/female incongruity. He envisioned a "great big kitchen in which things are always going wrong—milk boiling over, crockery getting smashed, toast burning, animals stealing. That was Purgatory, he knew, because the women had to learn to sit still and mind their own business; because the men had to learn to jump up and do something about it."[74]

Middle School students tiptoe into laughter about these taboo topics. They know that boys and girls are different, leading to fear, curiosity, desire, and humorous teasing. In an age of awkwardness, inquisitiveness, and bravado, laughter regarding gender allows them

to navigate the vagaries of difference and cope with their own uncer-
tainty. Few repress; most inquire, however sneakily.

On tendentious tendencies in excremental humor, Lewis did
imitate Voltaire once ("I am sitting in the smallest room of the house.
I have your letter before me; it will soon be behind me") in writing a
letter to his good friend, Arthur Greeves.[75] He wrote, "Can medita-
tion be combined with emptying of the bowels. What a saving of
time, especially for a constipated man like you."[76] The puckish boy in
many of us has not disappeared.

Rod Martin's Four Types of Humor

Psychologist Robert Provine contends that: "most laughter is not
a response to jokes or other formal attempts at humor," which should
be a grand relief to all teachers who feel gelato-challenged (the lack of
ability to evoke laughter).[77] Studying the Joke Proper, he found that less
than 2% of our laughter springs from intentional humor. The comic
classroom culture extends beyond slapstick and stand-up routines,
as one classroom does not aspire to be a workshop in telling jokes.[78]
In *The Art of Teaching with Humor*, author Teri Evans-Palmer argues
that, "teaching is a performance akin to stand-up comedy."[79] Yet, jokes
are not necessary for comic experiences, even though they add those
onions and spices that animate a salad. What a study of the jokes can
do for students is to help them identify their own style of humor.

The best place to help students understand what kind of humor
they practice is through the work of Canadian psychologist Rod
Martin. Martin outlined four overlapping humor styles: affiliative
humor, self-enhancing humor, self-defeating humor, and aggressive humor.[80] His questionnaire enables students to identify which
orientation(s) they fall into and then to assess what is benign and
what is injurious in their practice. One way to handle such creeping
and contagious darkness is to help students identify the tendencies
they favor. Martin's research on humor styles applies aptly to adolescents as he provides insights on dominant traits.

The affiliative or laughing at life is a positive ability to recognize how one views daily annoyances, foibles, even hypocrisies with a lighthearted grace, in which one makes others laugh. Facilitating relationships, its bonding allows a connection with others accentuating similarities, and establishes positive rapport with others. Self-enhancing humor provides a gentle humility, providing an indirect way to cope with challenges.

Self-effacing or self-mocking humor, sometimes translated as "hate-me-humor," invites self-deprecation where one makes light of oneself and expresses nonchalance. Many gifted students tend to embrace this. It also includes any defensive or nervous expressions of laughter, suggesting that the person does not take himself too seriously. Arnold Lobel depicted such self-effacing humor in his *Frog and Toad* series. He explained, "It seems to me the one thing that doesn't change much as we grow older is our sense of humor. I think a child's sense of humor and an adult's sense of humor are rather the same (except) our points of reference become larger. But the basics: we laugh at incongruity and we laugh at the lack of dignity. If a man's pants fall down, everybody laughs, children and adults."[81] When Toad and Frog go for a swim in *Frog and Toad are Friends*, Toad is afraid that others will laugh at him when he puts on his bathing suit. His friend Frog tries to protect his vanity, but Toad's insistence leads to a community of creatures laughing at his old-fashioned bathing suit.[82] So SpongeBob SquarePants rips his pants and finds he can laugh with others at his own silliness. However, he tries to exploit this comic mishap, so much that it becomes cringe-worthy and embarrassing.

After winning the NBA championship, Denver Nuggets star Nikola Jokić was interviewed about being drafted so low (and not even being selected during the television show) and now becoming the NBA Finals MVP. Jokić paused and grinned: "They didn't believe in the fat boy. It seems like it worked out. Don't bet against the fat boy."[83] Such self-effacing humor won over all audiences.

Young adolescents with low self-esteem tend to use self-defeating humors. They know that this type of humor will get others to laugh, however, continually talking about oneself in such a low manner may lead a child to believe they are worthless. These insecurities and vulnerabilities get picked up by aggressive students and may perpetuate the cycle of bullying. Bullies often focus on the other children they view as weak. A child with low self-esteem becomes an easy target. The more they are made fun of by themselves and others, the more these students believe what they are saying.

Put-down humor, which we will address more under Flippancy, comes at the expense of others, baring the teeth and demonstrating aggressive assertion of dominance or superiority over others. Its critical quality aims at manipulating and disparaging its targets. Its sour and bitter flavors strike as derision, contempt, and dismissal. Both self-enhancing humor and aggressive humor boost the self. In contrast, self-defeating humor and affiliative humor augment others, showing sensitivity and empathy. However, self-enhancing humor and affiliative humor provide benign relationships while aggressive and self-defeating humor styles injure the parties involved.

Part of the usefulness of Martin's categories is his self-assessment scale in his Humor Style Questionnaire that enables teachers and students to share in understanding their respective styles.[84] In fact, while also teaching math skills, the questionnaire enables students to see themselves from a fresh perspective, appreciate their peers' senses of humor, and laugh at themselves.

Tidbit

Have students read and fill out Martin's Humor Style Questionnaire and then ask if they do see themselves in the category that he predicts.[85] Group students based

on humor style and watch their surprise at who is in their group.

Recognition of incongruities in life and one's own self spark a sensational season of mental acuity. Students discover their own wit and that of their peers and find opportunities to experiment in both positive and negative ways. While Freudian and Hobbesian theories of laughter dealing with relief and superiority offer insights into the practice of student wit, many jokes blossom out of the recognition of incongruity. The crowning glory of bright and witty students comes as they recognize incongruous situations that provide opportunity for their creative laughter.

As Cheryl Mizerny astutely concludes, "Middle school students have a ready sense of humor. They are not yet so jaded that they are too cool to crack up at something corny. They have no filter and say any old thing that pops into their heads, often with unintentionally hysterical results between wanting to blend in to the crowd and wanting to be their authentic, quirky selves."[86]

Of course, quirky selves can turn cruel. The laughter of jokes, like all other good gifts, can be twisted and bent into evil. They can become the taboo humor of adolescent boys, sometimes smutty and cruel.

Basic curiosity about emerging sexuality propels boys to snicker and snigger. Now some joke about sex because it reveals many incongruities. Others look to humor as a way to talk about sex. Peer influence bonds many boys in exploring this new and seemingly dangerous and forbidden world through joking. Sex-related jokes stem from media like Tik Tok, *Beavis and Butthead*, *South Park*, and Adult Swim and abet not only a means to challenge authority, but a way to utilize raunchy humor to assert one's independence or attract attention from peers. Whenever it can, such bawdy jesting will poke itself into an innocent discussion.

The humor can also help them cope with awkward situations. Humor helps to navigate the rapid complexities of their changing bodies and their mercurial emotions, making this mystery less intimidating. A less obvious use of jokes evolves as a way to excuse shame or other vices. Lewis's Screwtape writes of this danger:

> If a man simply lets others pay for him, he is "mean"; if he boasts of it in a jocular manner and twits his fellows with having been scored off, he is no longer "mean" but a comical fellow. Mere cowardice is shameful; cowardice boasted of with humorous exaggerations and grotesque gestures can be passed off as funny. Cruelty is shameful— unless the cruel man can represent it as a practical joke. A thousand bawdy, or even blasphemous, jokes do not help towards a man's damnation so much as his discovery that almost anything he wants to do can be done, not only without the disapproval but with the admiration of his fellows, if only it can get itself treated as a Joke.[87]

It will lead to the most toxic kind of laughter in the classroom, flippancy, which is where we turn in our next chapter.

Chapter Six

On Flippancy ~
Descent into Darkness

NOT ALL REPORTS ON HUMOR ARE SO CHEERY. Back in 1811, Richard Hurd complained that laughter "obscures truth, hardens the heart, and stupefies the imagination."[1] C. S. Lewis recognizes that anything that demands reverence, risks ridicule, including laughter. Laughter begins to be a demon the moment it begins to be a god. G. K. Chesterton notices that "two types of me laugh when they are alone: He is either confiding the joke to God or confiding it to the Devil."[2] Flippancy cultivates an atmosphere of superiority and conniving. It gathers an inner ring, a coterie of like-minded cads, who are "in the know."

Middle and High School laughter turns darker and more aggressive as the students move through these uncertain liminal years. Humor frequently descends into cruelty, ridicule, and ultimately bullying. As students wrestle with issues of identity, alienation, and community, they find negative responses easier to express than more vulnerable, positive, and sensitive communication. As laughter deteriorates into expressions of meanness, students lose much of the positive, affiliative experiences that laughter can bring. This chapter explores the signs and habits of such anti-social expressions, particularly the variety that Lewis called Flippancy. He saw its first buds sprouting from small cheeky boys, such that "half an hour in the society of a French thirteen-year-old makes most of us feel that there is something to be said for fagging after all."[3] Better to prune or nip the mean, little, weedy sprouts in the bud.

The frivolous lack of respect with its underlying cruelty forms the foundation of flippancy. Lewis shows children examples of flippancy in its undesirable meanness and its deserved consequences. Tormenting begins almost immediately as the White Witch looks at Edmund and declares him "an idiot, whatever else you may be."[4] Name-calling smacks of verbal bullying, a negative infection imitated by Edmund with his sister. The primary behavioral model of humor, however, comes through a façade of friendly banter. When the Witch's dwarf offers Edmund the tasty, but addictive Turkish Delight, he does so with a "bow and a smile; not a very nice smile."[5] Later, with Edmund desperately seeking food and drink, the Dwarf brings an iron bowl with water and a dry hunk of bread. "He grinned in a repulsive manner as he set them down on the floor beside Edmund and said, 'Turkish Delight for the little Prince. Ha! Ha! Ha!'"[6]

Early scenes in the Chronicles provide two fundamental elements of this little demonic habit of belittling. First appears the distorted smile, what may crack into a smirk. Chesterton champions the laugh over the smile. He throws three strikes against the Victorian smile. First, it can "unobtrusively turn into the sneer."[7] Second, the smile remains an individual and even secretive act. Finally, controlled and guarded, the smile spoils with a tinge of cynicism. In contrast, laughter lives most robustly in communal, social, gregarious, and fun spheres.

The smile can be controlled, remain dignified, and turn into a smirk. It can become condescending and wicked. It can become a weapon to wound rather than an ointment to heal. The unguarded innocence of laughter soars with the ancient winds of inspiration; "it unfreezes pride and unwinds secrecy; it makes men forget themselves in the presence of something greater than themselves; something (as the common phrase goes about a joke) that they cannot resist."[8] The cold smile sneers in its spitefulness. The smile is the product of wit while laughter is the child of mirth, for "A laugh is like a love affair in that it carries a man completely off his feet."[9] A smile is like a seduction, in that it teases and tempts, but does not love.

The Witch, herself, flatters and treacherously confides in a duped Edmund as she conspires to capture his siblings: "You needn't tell them about me. It would be *fun* to keep it a secret between us two, wouldn't it?" (italics mine)[10] Even when Edmund begs for more Turkish Delight, she withholds it, and says with a laugh, "you must wait until next time."[11] Her specious laughter hides a manipulative power over which she holds the boy. When she later hears that the other Son of Adam and Daughters of Eve arrived at the house of the Beavers, "a slow cruel smile" spreads over the Witch's face.[12]

Secondly, the infection of laughter, even bullying laughter, can be seen when Edmund echoes that condescending laugh a little later when he denies being in Narnia. As John Hoover and Glenn Olson argued in "Sticks and Stones May Break Their Bones," Edmund practices a form of teasing that equates to bullying.[13] He gives a superior look at his little sister and then, with a "little snigger" says, "Oh, yes, Lucy and I have been playing—pretending that all her story about a country in the wardrobe is true. Just for *fun*, of course" (italics mine); then Peter reprimands him for "jeering and nagging at her."[14] Later, when Edmund finds himself in a courtyard of statues, he first feels terror; then realizing they are only made of stone, he jeers and mocks them, even penciling a mustache and a pair of spectacles onto one of the fierce-looking lions. As such, he experiences some of what Sigmund Freud explained as relief, a release from taboos and of challenging authority. In spite of his silly actions, the stone lion stands nobly in the moonlight and Edmund gets no "fun out of jeering at it."[15]

The nadir of flippancy occurs at what Michael Screech called

Laughter at the Foot of the Cross.[16] Having Aslan in her grasp, the Witch again gives a wild, fierce laugh. It is not one of relief from fear, but of specious victory, a shriek of unfounded triumph, mocking him as a fool. When the Witch calls the creatures to shave the shackled lion, they emit "another roar of mean laughter."[17] Then, as the soldiers had mocked Jesus and laid a crown of thorns upon His head, the ogres and others sneer at Aslan. The scene recalls something of the artistry of Fra Angelico's *Mocking of the Christ* (1445) in which bodiless hands beat and spit accosts Jesus, and the grotesque characters in Hieronymus Bosch's *Christ Carrying the Cross* (1480), or Lucas Cranach's *The Mocking of Christ* (1553) as they wag their tongues and laugh through their bulbous noses.[18]

They mock him as only being a great cat, nothing to be afraid of; in fact, they jeer, taunting him with "'Puss, Puss! Poor Pussy,' and 'How many mice have you caught today, Cat?'" and in lieu of vinegar, "Would you like a saucer of milk, Pussums?"[19] They escalate their tortures, hitting him, spitting on him, and unrelentingly jeering him. The laughter seems all cackles and screeches.

What is curious about flippancy as a model of laughter is that Lewis employs it not only among villains, but also among the children protagonists themselves. Edmund's early flippancy prepares us for that of Eustace, Jill, and numerous characters. Those who come to know Aslan begin to realize the twisted nature of such laughter. Researchers who investigate the topic of laughter and bullying find that mean-spirited ridicule, i.e. bullying laughter, generates fear in *gelotophobes*, those who fear being laughed at and significantly aggravates a temptation to respond aggressively.[20] Embarrassing situations aggravate the possibility of *katagelasticism* (the pleasure in laughing at others, or even more darkly, at laughing at their misfortune as in the German word *schadenfreude*) which increases with observing someone else's discomfort. Victims, however, retreat or retaliate, and if they have no sarcastic verbal skills with which to compete, physical violence may ensue.

Flippancy, for Lewis, was that laughter that causes social pain; it often excludes others from the inner ring, by a raised eyebrow or slight smirk.[21] Flippancy involves psychologist Rod Martin's categories of aggressive and put-down humor that mocks and ridicules.[22] Screwtape observed that it is very economical:

> Only a clever human can make a real Joke about virtue, or indeed about anything else; any of them can be trained to talk *as if* virtue were funny. Among flippant people, the Joke is always assumed to have been made. No one actually makes it; but every serious subject is discussed in a manner which implies that they have already found a ridiculous side to it (italics in original).[23]

For Lewis, the habit of Flippancy contains no Joy and it "deadens, instead of sharpening, the intellect; and it excites no affection between those who practice it."[24]

Students often describe "Middle School humor" as mean, immature, and teasing. Cringe culture makes students feel inferior if they express passion or excitement about a particular topic. Some attempts at humor are thwarted because a child is called "cringe" or "extra." This discourages humorous participation in the classroom and has a negative impact on the culture. Teachers can discourage flippancy by reacting favorably to honest attempts at positive humor—jokes, puns, goofiness, and creativity—while making it clear that flippancy will not be tolerated. This may require forced smiles and laughter, but all for the benefit of humorous risk-taking.

Tidbit

Study the use of cruel and mean humor in history, literature, media, and politics. Inquire as to what students

think the effects of that flippancy may have been. Share examples that have hurt others. What were the consequences of using cruel laughter?

The group in the Chronicles most like flippant Middle School boys (and girls) is the faction of bad dwarfs. "The Dwarfs are for the Dwarfs," they sneer.[25] They refuse to be made fools of by committing themselves only to themselves. They mock the promise of rescue with elitist cynicism. They refuse to be made part of a joke, even if the joke is for their benefit. And be assured, Chesterton warns, that if a man cannot make a fool of himself, the effort might be quite superfluous.[26] These dwarfs in *The Last Battle* become stubborn fools, creatures that look "at one another with grins; sneering grins, not merry ones."[27] As they choose their own destruction, Aslan rues, "They will not let us help them. They have chosen cunning instead of belief. Their prison is only in their minds, yet they are in that prison; and so afraid of being taken in that they cannot be taken out."[28]

Misguided wit is the father of the twisted smile, the sneer, scorn, and sarcasm; however, mirth is the mother of laughter. When challenged by their aggressive humor, the wits employ the "just kidding" defense. However, as the proverb cautions: "Like a maniac who shoots flaming arrows . . . so is a person who deceives his neighbor, and says, 'Was I not joking?'" (Prov. 26:18–19, NASB). Flippancy jibes can stab and break bones even with a steely smile. Unless the smile opens itself up, it will hold in laughter that will fester, grow stale, and die.

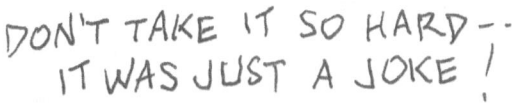

FIG 6. Lewis warned that the British take their sense of humor so very seriously. "Humour is for them the all-consoling and (mark this), the all-excusing, grace of life.[29] If one twits his fellow, he can excuse himself for being a comic, jocular fellow. (Courtesy of John Lawing. Used with permission)

In flippancy, one recognizes that laughter, like cheese, eggs, oysters, and blind dates, can go bad. Human laughter can be wicked because the human heart is wicked. "The human being is the only animal that blushes— or needs to," Mark Twain tartly notes; "But you have to remember that we were made at the end of a week's work."[30] Such laughter leads to aggressive behaviors like teasing and bullying, where weaker students become victims of others.[31]

In *The Screwtape Letters*, Lewis explores the relations between the fallen human condition and humor. Humor, he wrote, involves a sense of proportion and seeing oneself from the outside. The comic muse teaches us to see ourselves humbly as others see us, to have a perspective outside our own myopic view. John Morreall emphasizes how humor jolts us with a "sudden change of mental state—a cognitive shift, that would be disturbing under normal circumstances, that is if we took it seriously."[32] Humor provides a mental flexibility and enables an escape from what economist Thorstein Veblen once called *Trained Incapacity*[33] or what Henri Bergson defined as comedy in our resemblance to "the mechanical encrusted upon the living."[34] We are conditioned, stuck in a certain manner of repetitive behavior or acting like machines without thinking. We are too similar to Randle McMurphy in Ken Kesey's *One Flew over the Cuckoo's Nest*. As he enters the insane asylum, McMurphy notices: "That's the first thing that got me about this place, that there wasn't anybody laughing. I haven't heard a real laugh since I came through that door . . . Man, when you lose your laugh, you lose your footing."[35] Neil Postman, author of *Amusing Ourselves to Death*, observes that children enter school as question marks and leave as periods.[36] One needs to keep inquiring, asking questions, seeing from fresh perspectives, and needs to develop a sense of humor that will break their mechanical Trained Incapacity. It liberates us from established habits. It helps one escape the Cuckoo's Nest.

Tidbit

First, have students play charades and imitate mechanical objects (e.g. a vacuum cleaner, a coffee pot, a lawn mower, etc.). Ask where Bergson is right about people acting like machines. Second, identify what students

believe may be their "trained incapacities" regarding humor. Have they learned to laugh at themselves? Then ask students to try this experiment: First, lift your right foot off the floor and make Clockwise Circles. Now, while continuing this movement, draw the number '6' in the air with your Right Hand. The foot will change direction. Have them reflect on where they are stuck in life.

We will be happier when we see and confess our shortcomings. H. Allen Smith defines a humorist as a "fellow who realizes, first, that he is no better than anybody else, and second, that nobody else is either."[37] As the great nineteenth century humorist observes, "Man is the only animal that laughs and weeps: for he is the only animal that is struck with the difference between what things are, and what they ought to be."[38]

Laughter, like any other good gift, can be corrupted, bent, spoiled, and ruined. Rotted laughter is thus like "Lilies that fester [that] smell far worse than weeds."[39] As we mentioned, laughter becomes demonic the moment it begins to be a god. If we make laughter a god and worship it, it takes its own revenge upon us. It dies. Laughter is not enough to sustain us. It must be recognized as a simple gift; not the gift of life itself.

Lewis warns of the laughter of Flippancy. Flippancy jokes about goodness, virtue, justice. It is cruelty disguised as joking. Our throats are like open sepulchers, graves where dead laughter exists. The weed of flippancy grows in the soil of superiority and pride. Its grubby root is in meanness; in fact, one of the best movies to capture it is *Mean Girls*. Over a cup of coffee and a sneering wink and a rolling of the eyes, we mock others. We laugh, but know we should be repenting.

FIG 7. Unfortunately, students not only imitate the gentle laughter of the teacher, but the more mocking tendencies as well. (Courtesy of John Lawing. Used with permission)

Much of this malign laughter oozes out of what the Germans call *Schadenfreude*, which as we mentioned earlier means taking pleasure in someone else's misfortune, derived from *Schaden* (damage, harm) and *Freude* (joy). We can easily confess that we chuckle when friends mess up or suffer. It satisfies those who believe in the superiority theory of laughter, that our laughter is simply derision at others, de-rising them. There are even

Schadenfreude greeting cards: Glad you flunked. Glad you have gas. Glad your cat died.

Students learn the laughter of vice as well as virtue from their elders. Dutch artist Jan Steen's merry and didactic 1670 painting of a Jacob Cats' proverb, "As the Old Sing, So Pipe the Young," illustrates how mimicry of mirth trickles down from parents and teachers to the young.[40] In his wildly chaotic "classroom," the laughing father (Steen himself) instructs his child how to smoke a pipe. We teach what we are. If we have no good laughter, neither will our students. Thus, it behooves us to eschew the laughter of mocking and cruelty. A bad example leads to bad conduct.

Beginning in Middle School, such derision becomes a primary mode of self-defense. Humor functions as a weapon or as a means to be terminally cool. Smart alecks and mean girls take center stage. The challenge for educators is to redirect that cruel laughter into something positive. One encouraging story came out of a private school in Washington State in a report of a unique Middle School problem. A number of twelve-year-old girls were beginning to use lipstick, applying it on in the bathroom.

> That was fine, but after they applied their lipstick, they would press their lips to the mirror leaving dozens of little lip prints. Every night the maintenance man would remove them and the next day the girls would put them back. Finally, the principal decided that something had to be done. She called all the girls to the bathroom and met them there with the maintenance man.
>
> She explained that all these lip prints were causing a major problem for the custodian who had to clean the mirrors every night. To demonstrate how difficult it had been to clean the mirrors, she asked the maintenance man to show the girls how much effort was required.
>
> He took out a long-handled squeegee, dipped it in the toilet,

and cleaned the mirror with it. Since then, there have been no lip prints on the mirror. There are teachers, and then there are educators.[41]

Like weeds, harmful laughter will continually sprout in the classroom. The challenge now is to plant benign laughter into the fertile field. "The real way of mending a man's taste," Lewis wrote, "is not to denigrate his present favorites but to teach him how to enjoy something better."[42] The first step is to encourage a practice of playfulness.

Chapter Seven

Tricks of the Trade

For c. s. lewis, a central key to fruitful education emerges out of his attack on modern education. His experience taught him that for every "one pupil who needs to be guarded from a weak excess of sensibility, there are three who need to be awakened from the slumber of cold vulgarity."[1] The true task of the educator is "not to cut down jungles but to irrigate deserts."[2] Few experiences water and refresh an arid and dusty soul as laughter.

Knowing there are different kinds of laughter and humor styles is one thing. Teaching laughter and establishing habits of comic perception is another. Researchers investigated seven types of humor (funny stories, funny comments, professional humor, puns, cartoons, and riddles) as generally positive in the college classroom.[3] They also speculated that four types of instructor humor (sarcasm, sexual humor, ethnic humor, and aggressive/hostile humor) negatively affected students. Such general wisdom reflects common sense. While many view jokes as one of the least effective ways to elicit laughter, researcher Emma Philips finds that students enjoy "slapstick comedy the funniest with the bathroom humor in a close second."[4] Yet, she observes that students had a hard time settling down after watching the video clip, concluding that perhaps these types of humor are not the most appropriate for the classroom.

Let us start at the ground level. If you do not smile when you enter a classroom, you have already lost a significant advantage. That basic Zygomatic smile can melt antagonistic students and encourage introverted ones. One can take several steps to develop the maximum effectiveness of a simple smile. You do not need to feel funny or even be happy to smile. It is an act of the will and a habit of presentation. By enacting the Duchenne smile, by putting on a cheerful face, you will come to feel it. This is not simply the power of positive thinking, but a recognition of the effects of your body upon your mood. Some days this Sisyphean task will not seem possible, even with the most earnest of comic efforts, but continue to exercise the smile. (In fact, in some seasons, none of these habits will help. We are mired in sin and in a broken world and it takes something transcendent to correct it.)

Second, become comfortable with smiling. This does not mean practicing in front of a mirror or looking down at a stream of water like Narcissus, but of stretching those facial muscles early in the morning. Then imagine a situation of joy before you arrive. Psychologist Leo Widrich recommends that before engaging another person in conversation, one should "visualize someone they deeply love, or recall an event that brought them deep satisfaction and joy. It's such an easy exercise, and we train people to do it in our workshops."[5] Following closely, practice smiling. Walking down a path, do not be stuck on your iPhone, but look around you with a smile as you greet people. Mother Teresa wisely observed that, "We shall never know all the good that a simple smile can do."[6] Smiles shape other people's lives more than we imagine.

Third, for teachers, find your laughing place. In the African tradition of trickster tales, the clever Br'er Rabbit finds himself captured by the cunning Br'er Fox and the dim-witted Br'er Bear (think administrators) and about to be roasted over a fire. For a final request, he asks if he can visit his "laughin' place."[7] Hoodwinked, the two follow him into a hive of bees that proceed to sting his captors. As they run away screaming, Br'er Rabbit doubles over with laughter. When stress and fatigue become enemies, a teacher needs to find her place of repose, of peace, of joy. It may be with another colleague or with a prayer, but one needs the space and time to regain perspective.

Fourth, develop your unique playfulness style. In a study comparing teachers' and children's playfulness, Shulamit Pinchover concludes that "Individuals who are playful are typically funny, humorous, spontaneous, and are more likely to act in a playful manner by joking, teasing, clowning, and being silly. Existing studies show that adults' playfulness is related to well-being, sense of happiness, relationship satisfaction, and higher self-estimates of ingenuity and creativity."[8] What do you enjoy about teaching? What aspects of your students' discovery and learning pump you with endorphins? Studies demonstrate how social laughter triggers positive hormonal releases; one should find ways to invite such laughter.[9] Focus upon cultivating that laughter among your students.

Fifth, as first impressions last at least a week or two, before the students really get to know you, your first classes matter. One way to introduce yourself with unexpected humor is by scripting an opening dialogue read as a Readers' Theater between teacher and students. The script can prepare students for the class and let them know your expectations. Weave incongruous bits with dull information into a comic drama that maps out what you expect of them, with a few digressions.

Sixth, if you are not too weary with too many directions, enable students to see the humor in what they read (and watch) in their assignments. Where do characters in the stories laugh? What do they laugh at? Early in Chapter 5 in *Moby Dick*, Ishmael looks at his sly and grinning landlord and reflects,

> However, a good laugh is a mighty good thing, and rather too scarce a good thing: the more's the pity. So, if any man, in his own proper person, afford stuff for a good joke to anybody, let him not be backward, but let him cheerfully allow himself to spend and be spent in that way. And the man that

has anything bountifully laughable about him be sure there is more in that man than you perhaps think for.[10]

Ask what this says about looking at differences among people and celebrating those differences with good humor. Even in *Beowulf*, everyone the title character meets seems impressed with his bravado. Even the sea watchman for Herot loves him: "A greater ne'er saw I of warriors in the world than is one of you."[11] Ask students if they would talk about strangers in this way and see them giggle.

In *A Christmas Carol*, Charles Dickens repeatedly affirms the role that laughter has even in desperate times, for "There is nothing in the world so irresistibly contagious as laughter and good humor . . . It is a fair, even-handed, noble adjustment of things, that while there is infection in disease and sorrow, there is nothing in the world so irresistibly contagious as laughter and good humor."[12] And later, adding, "Nothing ever happened on this globe, for good, at which some people did not have their fill of laughter in the onset; and knowing that such as these would be blind anyway, he thought it quite as well that they should wrinkle up their eyes in grins, as have a malady in the less attractive forms."[13]

The humor of Mark Twain bursts forth in his novels like *Tom Sawyer*, in which an "old man laughed loud and joyously, shook up the details of his anatomy from head to foot, and ended by saying that such a laugh was money in a–man's pocket, because it cut down the doctor's bill like everything."[14] What might such laughter look like? Can students imitate it?

When students study Homer's *Odyssey*, they catch the joke of Odysseus calling himself "Noman."[15] As the giant screams to his neighbors "Noman" has blinded me, they all laugh.[16] More than a trivial pun or verbalism, G. K. Chesterton shows how the joke is in

the gigantic image of the raging Cyclops, roaring as if to rend the mountains, after being defeated by something so simple and so small. This example is worth noting; as representing what is really the fun of all the fairy-tales; the notion of something apparently omnipotent made impotent by some tiny trick. This fairy-tale idea is undoubtedly one of the primitive fountains from which flows the long winding stream of historic humor. When Puss in Boots persuades the boastful magician to turn into a mouse and be eaten, it almost deserves to be called wit.[17]

Tidbit

Seek and find the pearls of laughter in literary works and let the students squeeze out the humor for sheer pleasure. While more challenging in some texts than others, students can always find some comic tidbit.

Seventh, know your audience. Familiarize yourself with students' interests and humor. Eliciting laughter in the halls of academia is a risky business. For starters, the humor of your generation may not resonate with that of your students. How many classes have I spent on jests about age or marriage to millennials, only to have them fall as flat as a manhole cover? And laughter without an echo is a quickly evaporating sound. Yet, we know that many attempts at creating humorous messages lead to laughter and generally produce a positive influence in the classroom. Old dogs do need to learn new tricks. What do your students laugh at? To whom are they listening and watching that cause them to laugh? Also, know what frustrations and anxieties they are experiencing (like the myth of Sisyphus trying to roll a rock up a hill over-and-over-again), or if they have or a simple lack of motivation. Where do they go for rejuvenation? What tickles their fancies?

Eighth, various techniques easily provide opportunities for playfulness in the classroom. Such literary bits include Alliteration, Oxymorons, and Acronyms. When students create a three-word alliteration of their names or answer, "how are you?" with three alliterative words, they tend to hone imaginative and comic skills. An oxymoron playfully presents a figure of speech in which two terms appear contradictory, such as George Carlin's classic "jumbo shrimp" or Lewis's "spiritual animal."[18] A humorous turn of phrase helps students connect and remember important information.

Direct students to play linguistic games with their own names. Co-founders of the International Society for Humor Studies, the wonderfully comic couple, Don and Alleen Nilsen published their pioneering work on *Names and Naming in Young Adult Literature*, investigating literary onomastics, studying the history and origin of proper names and personal names.[19] Their foundational work, *The Language of Humor: An Introduction*, provides one of the most enjoyable roller-coaster rides of laughter across the disciplines, including clowning and children's linguistic games.[20]

The use of acronyms as words formed from the initial letters of other words, especially as seen in military and bureaucratic systems, does help recall humorous information more quickly and easily. These literary elements allow for simple, humorous items within the context of the class that students can use to remember important information. Long after they have left your classroom, students hold onto such mnemonic devices that linger in the memory, even longer than you may.

Ninth, as we mentioned earlier, music and singing not only break up prosaic lessons, but enable students to learn indirectly. Sing-a-longs refresh dull moments, even a classic like Shirley Ellis's Name Game (avoiding, of course, the name Chuck) will invite full class participation. If one is so talented, one can even rewrite popular songs with lyrics (no matter how bad) that contain relevant lessons. One can also identify a class song and return to it just before a weekend or in a desperate class situation. One of our authors observed how Drake and Taylor Swift songs can turn into one of the best prompts for novels in her classroom.

While aware of your own frustrations, limitations, and fears, still seek to engender a *climate of humor*. Allow breaks for play, even if that means just standing, stretching, swaying, or clapping. In one college course, several students were not reading the assignments. Thus, the professor initiated a Squid Game, where all the students stood at attention until they had answered a question from the assigned readings. Within one class period, students had begun reading.

Think of creative ways to assign learning outside of class. In a course on Communication and Laughter, the professor tried a Funny Hat Day and an opportunity to imitate another teacher's eccentricities. Once, we handed out Comic Face Cookies and assigned students to photograph themselves and their cookies in a humorous situation. The presentations of their work brought the most raucous laughter of the semester, particularly where the Cookie murdered a beloved pet dog.

One can also incorporate cameo shots of students to insert on an early introductory PowerPoint lecture that deals with facial imagery, the Duchenne smile, and humor research. The advantage of putting *all* their faces on one PowerPoint slide is that each student will only look at himself or herself, cringe, and laugh, in what we call the Comic Narcissist Effect. No individual stands out, but all are able to see their own vanity and folly. Rather than being mortified, when they realize that they are not looking at anyone else's image, they laugh realizing no one is looking at theirs either.

Finally, do not feel the need to create humor yourself, but encourage the humor of others. Encourage the wit and humor of the students to bring fresh air into the learning environment. Affirm those students who contribute spontaneous laughter. Respond to student attempts at humor with laughter. Funny events occur in classroom environments and situations frequently, so teachers do not need to be funny themselves. We just need to make sure that we recognize and acknowledge when something funny happens, instead of ignoring it. Research shows that by incorporating laughter in the classroom, students learn how to use humor, with teachers providing students avenues to learn reasoning, listening, and socially appropriate expression.

Conclusion

"THERE WAS A CHILD WENT FORTH EVERY DAY," penned Walt Whitman, "And the first object he looked upon and received with wonder or pity or love or dread, that object he became, And that object became part of him for the day or a certain part of the day . . . or for many years or stretching cycles of years."[1]

For students reading *The Chronicles of Narnia*, there is an opportunity to look upon the objects of laughter, and to become like those objects. The stories model types and valences of laughter, showing the mean bullying of flippancy and its consequences, pointing to the quick wit of jests and jokes, inviting children to laugh robustly in their play and enjoyment of life, and preparing them for moments of joy and gladness that transcends one's daily routine. Such species of laughter overlap, of course, but each resonates with those who look upon such phenomena.

Inspired by Johann Wolfgang von Goethe's idea that the "directions taken by a person's laughter are one of the best clues to his character,"[2] James Sully contemplated how one might gauge a child's humor and teach the young to laugh. How would one examine the "quality of the 'humour' expressed"?[3] He has no satisfactory answer. On the other hand, the writer who most influenced C. S. Lewis on this topic, G. K. Chesterton, reminds us of a necessary condition: "Laughter has something in it in common with the ancient winds of faith and inspiration; it unfreezes pride and unwinds secrecy; it makes men forget themselves in the presence of something greater than themselves; something (as the common phrase goes about a joke) that they cannot resist."[4] When a child enters *The Chronicles of Narnia*, she loses herself, and observing her new literary friends laughing, picks up the contagion and laughs with them.

What we have sought to do, however simply, is to remind ourselves that teachers can help students become agents of their own healthy laughter. Of course, learning standards must be met and time may feel too short for these things, but learning cannot happen without a positive classroom community. It may be a challenge for a student to learn to laugh well, even as it may be hard for an "egg to turn into a bird; it would be a jolly sight harder for a bird to learn to fly while remaining an egg."[5] Our students are like eggs at present and they "cannot go on indefinitely being just an ordinary, decent egg."[6] They "must be hatched or go bad."[7] Our challenge is to hatch humor in the hearts and minds of our students. In his *Abolition of Man*, Lewis reminds us that education invites us to initiate students into life rather than "condition" or indoctrinate them. The old traditions, he writes, "dealt with its pupils as grown birds deal with young birds when they teach them to fly; the new deals with them more as the poultry-keeper deals with young birds—making them thus or thus for purposes of which the birds know nothing."[8] Teachers must teach young birds how to fly, to laugh, to sing, to whistle, or at least to chirp.

One last moment takes us back to the droll, self-reflexive, portrait of the professor. Lewis's doppelganger, Professor Diggory, explains to his fellow saints in *The Last Battle*, that

> "It's all in Plato, all in Plato: bless me, what *do* they teach them at these schools!" The older ones laughed. It was exactly like the sort of thing they had heard him say long ago in that other world where his beard was gray instead of golden. He knew why they were laughing and joined in the laugh himself. But very quickly they all became grave again; for, as you know, there is a kind of happiness and

wonder that makes you serious. It is too good to waste on jokes.[9]

Our pedagogy of folly ends with one of our primary sources, namely Erasmus's *In Praise of Folly*. When the Dame descends from her teaching lectern, she squeezes in some last advice: "If we have been too cheeky or long-winded, remember you've been listening to Folly and a professor . . . Clap your hands, live well, and drink deep, most illustrious disciples of Folly."[10] For Alice in Wonderland, the Cheshire Cat leaves in a most appropriate way: It sat and chatted, then "vanished quite slowly, beginning with the end of the tail and ending with the grin, which remained sometime after the rest of it had gone."[11] We hope that as our students leave the classroom and slowly vanish into the day, that the Duchenne grin will linger and be the last thing to go.

Appendix

A Zygomatic Exercise Scripted Plan

This exercise is written in a lesson format to help teachers guide students through a deductive exploration of the physical and anatomical components of laughter. It is a great first-week-of-school activity, and it can also be used in physical education classes. Once students are familiar with the terminology, this can be used to give students a brain break that encourages laughter.

SAY: First, we will practice the zygomaticus major. This muscle connects the corner of your mouth with your cheek bone. Let's stretch it with a polite fake smile—a smile without involving the eyes. This is the smile I get when I try to tell jokes.

Teacher models a polite fake smile and students copy.

SAY: Next is the orbicularis oculis (Teacher may pause and work with students to identify the Latin roots of these words. This can be done throughout the exercise). These are the muscles around the eyes that show emotion. The orbicularis oculis is the reason we can tell someone is smiling when their mouth can't be seen. Now, squint for as long as possible at a peer. Let's see who can do this the longest. (This should get students laughing!)

Students squint at each other, and teacher times them.

SAY: Another reason people lovingly gaze into each other's eyes is the dilation of the pupils, the little black dot in everyone's eyes. We are more attracted to larger pupils. That's why romantic restaurants have bad lighting. Partner up and stare into each other's eyes. Take turns closing your eyes for about ten seconds and then quickly opening them. You should see your partner's pupils shrink in size as they open their eyes.

Give students time to practice gazing at each other's pupils.

SAY: Moving on up, let's talk about foreheads. During laughter and smiling, the eyebrows lift and the forehead opens up. Look back at your partner and smile, focusing on each other's foreheads and eyebrows. What movements occur?

Have students practice smiling and share their observations.

SAY: On the lower end of your face is the platisma, the lower lip and neck muscles. These help you create a wide mouth smile that stretches your lip down to show your teeth. When you smile widely with the platisma and raise your eyebrows, you create a smile that looks a bit creepy. It's a great face to make if you want to sit alone at lunch or don't want to share a seat on the bus. Let's practice going back and forth between the frontal muscles, your forehead and eyebrows, and your platisma.

On your command, have students alternate between raised eyebrows and wide mouths. See how fast students can switch between frontal and platisma.

SAY: We have been focusing on the silent aspects of laughter. Now, let's get loud! Put your hands on your belly, the anatomical word is the abdomen. As you push in, say, "Ha, ha, ha!" Now, "He, he, he!" Now, "Ho, ho, ho!" Now, "Mwa, ha, ha!" (Teacher should add any other fun laughing styles of their choosing.)

SAY: Now, let's focus on laughter's impact on the rest of the body. Raise your hand if you have ever laughed so hard you rocked back and forth, slapped your knee, cried, slapped somebody else?

For this next part, have students stand in a circle.

SAY: Bend down toward your toes, then as you rise up laugh (even if it's fake) and raise your hands up over your head. Keep laughing and throw your head back. Then, sway like those balloon people you see at car dealerships.

See if students are still faux laughing and watch their laughter turn into real, jovial giggles. If they haven't, encourage them to look at one another and continue.

Endnotes

INTRODUCTION

[1] Desiderius Erasmus, *The Praise of Folly and Other Writings*, ed. Robert M. Adams (New York: W.W. Norton & Co., 1989).

[2] Erasmus, *The Praise of Folly*, 7.

[3] Erasmus, *The Praise of Folly*, 25.

[4] Plato, *Symposium in The Dialogues of Plato*, trans. Benjamin Jowett (New York: Encyclopedia Britannica, 1952), 173.

[5] Plato, *Philebus in The Dialogues of Plato*, 629.

[6] Katarzyna Jazdzewska, "Laughter in Plato's and Xenophon's Symposia" in *Plato and Xenophon: Comparative Studies*, ed. Gabriel Danzig (Leiden, Netherlands: Brill, 2018), 187–207.

[7] Aristotle, *Art of Rhetoric*, trans. J. H. Freese, Loeb Classical Library 193 (Cambridge, MA: Harvard University Press, 1959), II: 12.

[8] Aristotle, *Nicomachean Ethics*, trans. H. Rackham, Loeb Classical Library 73 (Cambridge, MA: Harvard University Press, 1994), IV: 8.

[9] Aristotle, *Poetics*, trans. W. Hamilton Fyfe, Loeb Classical Library 199 (Cambridge, MA: Harvard University Press, 1965), V: 1449a.

[10] Aristotle, *Poetics*, V: 1449a.

[11] Aristotle, *Nicomachean Ethics*, 8.

[12] Marcus Tullius Cicero, *How to Tell a Joke: An Ancient Guide to the Art of Humor*, trans. Michael Fontaine (Princeton, NJ: Princeton University Press, 2021), xvi.

[13] Joseph Epstein, "'How to Tell a Joke' Review: A Funny Thing Happened on the Way to the Forum," *The Wall Street Journal*, June 4, 2021, https://www.wsj.com/articles/how-to-tell-a-joke-review-a-funny-thing-happened-on-the-way-to-the-forum-11622821485.

[14] Marcus Tullius Cicero, *De Divinatione*, Book II, 58 (Loeb Classical Library, 1923), http://penelope.uchicago.edu/Thayer/E/Roman/Texts/Cicero/de_Divinatione/2*.html, 505.

[15] Marcus Tullius Cicero, *On the Orator*, Book II, trans. E. W. Sutton and H. Rackham, Loeb Classical Library 348 (Cambridge, MA: Harvard University Press, 1942), lxiii.

[16] Horace (Quintus Horatius Flaccus), *The Satires, Epistles, and Ars Poetica*, trans. A. S. Kline (Poetry in Translation, 2005), https://www.poetryintranslation.com/klineashoracesatepap.php.

[17] Horace, *The Satires*, I.X.14–15. "Ridicule usually / Cuts through things better, more swiftly, than force." A Roman soldier walks into a bar. He looks at the bartender and holds up two fingers in a V, and says, "Five please."

[18] Horace, *The Satires*, I.I.24–25.

[19] G. K. Chesterton, "On Dickens," *The Bookman*, February 1912, 41: 247.

[20] Parker Palmer, "The Heart of a Teacher: Identity and Integrity in Teaching," *Change Magazine* 29, no. 6 (1997): 14–21. A revised version appears as Chapter 1 in *The Courage to Teach: Exploring the Inner Landscape of a Teacher's Life* (San Francisco, CA: Jossey-Bass, 2007).

[21] John Meyer, *Understanding Humor through Communication* (Lanham, MD: Lexington Books, 2015), iii.

[22] Roald Dahl, *Matilda* (New York City, NY: Puffin, 2016), 67.

[23] Terry Lindvall, *Suprised by Laughter: The Comic World of C. S. Lewis* (Nashville, TN: Thomas Nelson, 1996).

[24] John Banas, Norah Dunbar, Dariela Rodriguez, and Shr-Jie Liu, "A Review of Humor in Educational Settings: Four Decades of Research," *Communication Education* 60, no. 1 (2011), https://doi.org/10.1080/03634523.2010.496867; See also "Should teachers be funny?" *National Communication Association*, February 1, 2011, https://www.natcom.org/communication-currents/should-teachers-be-funny.

[25] Melanie Booth-Butterfield, Steven Booth-Butterfield, and Melissa Wanzer, "Funny Students Cope Better: Patterns of Humor Enactment and Coping Effectiveness," *Communication Quarterly* 55, no. 3 (2007): 299–315. https://doi.org/10.1080/01463370701490232; R. L. Garner, "Humor in Pedagogy: How Ha-Ha Can Lead to Aha!" *College Teaching* 54, no. 1 (Winter 2006): 177–180, https://www.jstor.org/stable/27559255; Melissa Bekelja Wanzer, Ann Bainbridge Frymier, Ann M. Wojtaszczyk, and Tony Smith, "Appropriate and Inappropriate Uses of Humor by Teachers," *Communication Education* 55, no. 2 (2006): 178–196, https://doi.org/10.1080/03634520600566132.

[26] William Buskist, Jason Sikorski, Tanya Buckley and Bryan K. Saville, "Elements of Master Teaching" in *The Teaching of Psychology*, eds. Stephen F. Davis and William Buskist (Mahwah, NJ: Lawrence Erlbaum, 2002), https://www.psicopolis.com/psicopedia/boxpdf/teacingpsy.pdf# page=48.

[27] Buskist et al., "Elements of Master Teaching."

[28] Buskist et al., "Elements of Master Teaching," 33.

[29] Katherine K. Frankel, "Heard the One about the Teacher Who Thought He was a Comedian?" *The Times Educational Supplement*, 2009, 4870, 22.

[30] Frankel, "Heard the One About the Teacher," 22.

[31] Arthur Koestler, *The Act of Creation* (New York: Macmillan, 1964).

[32] John Morreall (ed.) *The Philosophy of Laughter and Humor* (Albany: State University of New York, 1987), 136.

[33] Robert Provine, *Laughter: A Scientific Study* (New York: Penguin, 2000), 9.

[34] C. S. Lewis, *God in the Dock* (Grand Rapids, MI: Eerdmans, 1970), 65–66.

[35] Gary Larsen, "The Far Side: Primate Studies—Two Way Mirror," Card Cow, https://www.cardcow.com/968800/far-side-primate-studies-two-way-mirror-gary-larson/.

CHAPTER ONE:
C. S. Lewis and Laughter

[1] Lewis's humor begins in the first line of his dedication to Lucy Barfield where, as an old bachelor professor, he confesses that in writing this story for her, he had "not realized that girls grow quicker than books." But he acknowledges that while she is older, there will come a day when "you will be old enough to start reading fairy tales again. You can then take it down from some upper shelf, dust it, and tell me what you think of it. I shall probably be too deaf to hear, and too old to understand a word you say, but I shall still be . . . your affectionate Godfather." *The Lion, the Witch and the Wardrobe* (New York: Macmillan, 1950). This is not the first humorous moment, however. Lewis scholar Kay Lindskoog once observed the classic understatement of Lewis introducing the three servants of the house keeping staff, whose names were "Ivy, Margaret and Betty, but they do not come into the story much." In fact, this is the only time they are mentioned in all the Chronicles.

[2] C. S. Lewis, *Out of the Silent Planet* (New York: Macmillan, 1965), 17.

[3] See Samuel Gonzalez, "The Screwtape Letters Narrated by John Cleese," Abridged Version, YouTube Playlist, last updated July 1, 2014, https://www.youtube.com/playlist?list=PLA8BAC9375345E6C7.

[4] "The vital force or impulse of life." *Merriam-Webster*, s.v. "élan vital (n.)," accessed August 21, 2024, https://www.merriam-webster.com/dictionary/%C3%A9lan%20vital

[5] Stephen Potter, *Sense of Humour* (New York: Henry Holt, 1954), 30. Potter appeared at the same time as Lewis on the BBC and produced a radio series on such topics as "How to Woo" and "How to Blow Your Own Trumpet."

[6] James M. Barrie, *Peter and Wendy* (London: Hodder and Stoughton, 1911), https://etc.usf.edu/lit2go/86/peter-pan/1537/chapter-3-come-away-come-away/.

[7] Terry Lindvall, "Freud and Lewis on Jokes, Humor, and Laughter," *CSL: The Bulletin of the New York C. S. Lewis Society*, Sept/Oct 2011, 42, no. 5, 1–10, 12–15; *Surprised by Laughter: The Comic World of C. S. Lewis* (Nashville, TN: Thomas Nelson, 1996).

[8] One of the most renowned of citations pops up in writer/director Preston Sturges's classic film about Hollywood and laughter, *Sullivan's Travels* (1941). In the film, the eponymous hero is a comedy film director who wants to direct serious films (e.g. *O Brother, Where Art Thou*) rather than comedies (e.g. *Ants in Your Pants, Part III*), but ends up on a chain gang in the south. On Sunday night, he and his fellow prisoners attend an African American church where they exhibit a Disney cartoon, *Playful Pluto*, which elicits laughter from the congregation of the oppressed. Sullivan discovers "There's a lot to be said for making people laugh. Did you know that that's all some people have? It isn't much, but it's better than nothing in this cockeyed caravan." The director's nickname is *Sully*, an homage by the director to this psychologist of laughter. See Donald Crafton, "Infectious Laughter" in *Funny Pictures*, eds. Daniel Goldmark and Charlie Keil (Berkeley, CA: University of California Press, 2011), 73.

[9] Unlike Lewis's supernatural orientation, Sully grounded his thought on wit and laughter on a secular (physiological, psychological, and social) foundation, more akin to (but divergent from) the philosophical notion of incongruity found in Immanuel Kant's "nullified expectation" and Arthur Schopenhauer's contradiction between perception and conception. For Sully, both philosophers have their proper, but limited, domain, as the complex phenomena of laughter invites multiple principles. James Sully, *An Essay*

in Laughter: Its Forms, Its Causes, Its Development and Its Value (London: Longmans, Green, and Company, 1902), 135.

[10] Sully takes on Freud's notions of jokes at its roots. He critiques Herbert Spencer's similar "idea that laughter is an escape of nervous energy which has suddenly been set free," and finds the "theory of a convenient waste-pipe arrangement" inadequate for understanding that joyous outburst which marks a "sudden accession of happy consciousness." Sully, *An Essay in Laughter*, 23.

[11] Sully, *An Essay in Laughter*, 1.

[12] Evagrius of Pontus, *On the Eight Thoughts (Capita Cognoscitiva)* 13, *Greek Ascetic Corpus*, trans. Robert E. Sinkewicz (Oxford: Oxford University Press, 2003). The Egyptian monk identified the eight (sic) deadly sins and their corresponding virtues. *Hilaritas* (or cheerfulness) countered acedia and melancholy.

[13] C. S. Lewis, *The Screwtape Letters* (New York: Macmillan, 1968), 50.

[14] C. S. Lewis, *A Grief Observed* (Minneapolis, MN: Seabury, 1961), 57; See also his discussion on coarse jokes in Lewis's *Miracles* (New York: Macmillan, 1947), 132. In *The Everlasting Man*, Chesterton argues that alone among all the animals, this strange creature called a human "is shaken with the beautiful madness called laughter; as if he had caught sight of some secret in the very shape of the universe hidden from the universe itself." *Selected Works of G. K. Chesterton* (San Francisco, CA: Ignatius Press, 1987). In Lewis's space story *Perelandra*, the hero Ransom flies to Venus and arrives with one side of his body tanned while the other remains leprous white. When the Green Lady, the Eve of the planet, first sees him, she laughs out loud and calls him "Piebald." The joke juxtaposes a jolly incongruity, where one sees the human as an amazing oxymoron, a "spiritual animal."

[15] C. S. Lewis, *Poems*, ed. Walter Hooper (Orlando, FL: Harcourt Brace Jovanovich, 1964), 129.

[16] Sully, *An Essay in Laughter*, 194.

[17] Sully, *An Essay in Laughter*, 195.

[18] G. K. Chesterton, *All Things Considered* (Chester Springs, PA: Dufour, 1969), 26; For Chesterton, the quiddity of the ordinary provided supernatural pleasures. "A shower bath is not depressing; it is rather startling. And if it is exciting when a man throws a pail of water over you, why should it not also be exciting when the gods throw many pails?" *Tremendous Trifles* (London: Methuen, 1927), 267.

[19] Roald Dahl, *Matilda* (London: Puffin, 2016), https://online.pubhtml5.com/pien/hbbk/# p=1, 76–77; Lewis's works have had other critics as well, such as Harold Bloom who, while praising his literary scholarship, found the Chronicles to be "tendentious evangelical tale-telling." Of course, he confessed he really did not read them well. *Bloom's Modern Critical Views: C, S. Lewis* (New York: Chelsea House, 2006), 2.

[20] Dahl, *Matilda*, 63.

[21] Dahl, *Matilda*, 63.

[22] C. S. Lewis, *C. S. Lewis: Letters to Children*, eds. Lyle Dorsett and Marjorie Lamp Mead (New York: Macmillan, 1985), 37.

[23] Dahl, *Matilda*, 63. Dahl's humor is dark and much of it is tinged with sadism. For example, Matilda uses telekinetic powers to wreak revenge on her horrible, television-addicted, neglectful parents and deal with the cruel headmistress of a private school, Ms. Trunchbull, who disciplines one girl with pigtails by swinging her as an Olympic hammer event and throwing her across the playground. But some of this gallows humor will appear in Lewis's works as well.

[24] See *Laughter in Middle-earth: Humour in and around the Works of J. R. R. Tolkien*, eds. Thomas Honegger and Maureen F. Mann (Zurich: Walking Tree, 2016).

[25] See Terry Lindvall, *Surprised by Laughter* (Nashville, TN: Thomas Nelson, 1996).

[26] Alan Jacobs, "The Chronicles of Narnia" in *The Cambridge Companion to C. S. Lewis*, eds. Robert MacSwain and Michael Ward (Cambridge: Cambridge University Press, 2010), 265.

[27] In 1949, Chad Walsh noted that Lewis was writing a children's book (think fairy tale) "after the manner of E. Nesbit." *C. S. Lewis: Apostle to the Skeptics* (New York: Macmillan, 1949). Lewis enjoyed the thoroughly British characters (especially the fatuous grin of Mr. Toad) of Grahame's work and borrowed the realistic conversations and avuncular asides of Nesbit.

[28] C. S. Lewis, *On Stories and Other Essays* (Orlando, FL: Harcourt Brace Jovanovich, 1982), 14. Lewis says later that one does not "despise real woods because he has read of enchanted woods; the reading makes all real woods a little enchanted" (90).

[29] Jared Lobdell, *Eight Children in Narnia: The Making of a Children's Story* (Chicago, IL: Open Court, 2016), 4.

[30] Terry Mattingly, "C. S. Lewis for Children," 2005, http://www.leaderu.com/humanities/lewisforchildren.html.

[31] C. S. Lewis, "On Three Ways of Writing for Children," *On Stories*, ed. Walter Hooper (Eugene, OR: Harvest, 1982), 31.

[32] Lewis, "On Three Ways of Writing for Children," 32.

[33] See Victoria Davis, "'Interrupting Chicken' Teaches Kids Storytelling Outside the Lines," *Animation World Network*, AWN.com, November 18, 2022, https://www.awn.com/animationworld/interrupting-chicken-teaches-kids-storytelling-outside-lines.

[34] Lewis, "On Three Ways of Writing for Children," 32–33.

[35] Lewis, "On Three Ways of Writing for Children," 34.

[36] Lewis, "On Three Ways of Writing for Children," 34.

[37] Lewis, *C. S. Lewis: Letters to Children*, 34.

[38] William Makepeace Thackery, "A Grumble about the Christmas Books," *Fraser's Magazine* (January 1847), n.p.

[39] Lewis, "On Three Ways of Writing for Children," 35. When my daughter Caroline was about ten, we sat down to write a children's story. I asked her what the one thing was that she was afraid of losing. She answered, "My laugh." Thus, we wrote the tale of *The Girl Who Couldn't Laugh* (Hastings-on-Hudson, NY: Newington-Cropsey, 2012), about a young girl who was told to grow up and become sophisticated (which for Lewis was like the female human who prays to be made a normal twentieth century girl, which meant—to Screwtape—that she was asking "make me a minx, a moron, and a parasite.") (*Screwtape Letters*, 164). Fortunately, in our story, the girl's father brings in a mirror and revives the laughter of his daughter by enabling her to laugh at herself.

[40] Paul McGhee, *Understanding and Promoting the Development of Children's Humor* (Dubuque, IA: Kendall Hunt, 2002) and McGhee's *Humor: Its Origin and Development* (New York: W. H. Freeman, 1979).

[41] Lewis, *The Screwtape Letters*, 49–52.

[42] Doris Bergen, "Children's Humor and Giftedness," in *Encyclopedia of Humor Studies*, ed. Salvatore Attardo, vol. I (Los Angeles, CA: Sage, 2014), 120–121.

[43] C. S. Lewis, *Surprised by Joy* (Orlando, FL: Harcourt Brace Jovanovich, 1955).

[44] Lewis, *Surprised by Joy*, 45.

[45] Lewis, *Surprised by Joy*, 45.

[46] Lewis, *Surprised by Joy*, 46.

[47] Lewis, *Surprised by Joy*, 90.

[48] C. S. Lewis, *The Silver Chair* (New York: Macmillan, 1953), 40.

[49] C. S. Lewis, *Of Other Worlds: Essays and Stories* (Orlando, FL: Harcourt Brace Jovanovich, 1966), 34.

[50] Marti Southam, "An Important Cognitive and Social Skill in the Growing Child," *Humor Development* (July 29, 2009), 105–117; See also Karina Hess Zimmermann, "Children's Humor Stages," in *Encyclopedia of Humor Studies*, ed. Salvatore Attardo, vol. I (Los Angeles, CA: Sage, 2014), 126–127.

[51] Francoise Bariaud, "Chapter 1: Age Differences in Children's Humor," *Journal of Children in Contemporary Society* 20, no. 1–2 (1989): 15–45.

[52] Bariaud, "Chapter 1: Age Differences in Children's Humor," 15.

[53] Catherine Lyon, "Humour and the Young Child," *Research: Televizion* (2006): 4–9, https://izi.br.de/english/publication/televizion/19_2006_E/lyon.pdf.

[54] C. S. Lewis, *The Abolition of Man* (New York: HarperCollins, 1974), 23.

CHAPTER TWO:
Laughter in Middle School

[1] John Morreall, "Humor, Philosophy, and Education," *Educational Philosophy and Theory* 46, no. 2 (2014): 120–131.

[2] Hugh Foot and Antony Chapman, "The Social Responsiveness of Young Children in Humorous Situations," *Humor and Laughter Theory, Research, and Applications* (Oxfordshire: Routledge, 2017), 188.

[3] Karina Hess Zimmermann, "Children's Humor Research" in *Encyclopedia of Humor Studies*, ed. Salvatore Attardo, vol. I (Los Angeles, CA: Sage, 2014), 126.

[4] Arthur L. Costa and Bena Kallick, eds., *Habits of Mind Across the Curriculum: Practical and Creative Strategies for Teachers* (Alexandria, VA: Association for Supervision & Curriculum Development, 2009); Stephen R. Covey, *The 7 Habits of Highly Effective People: Powerful Lessons in Personal Change* (New York: Free Press, 2004).

[5] Serkan Demir and Ayca Konik, "Examining the Relationship between the Sense of Humor and the Social Exclusion Perceived by Gifted and Talented Students," *Shanlax International Journal of Education* 9, no. 2 (March 2021): 60–67.

[6] John Banas, Norah Dunbar, Dariela Rodriguez, and Liu, Shr-Jie, "Should Teachers be Funny?" *National Communication Association*, February 1, 2011, https://www.natcom.org/ communication-currents/should-teachers-be-funny.

[7] G. K. Chesterton, *Orthodoxy* (Toronto, ON: Doubleday, 1956), 121.

[8] Drew Appleby, "Using Humor in the College Classroom: The Pros and the Cons," *Psychology Teacher Network*, February 2018, https://www.apa.org/ed/precollege/ptn/2018/02/ humor-college-classroom.

[9] *School of Rock*, directed by Richard Linklater (Paramount Studios, 2003).

[10] John Banas, "A Review of Humor in Educational Settings: Four Decades of Research," *Communication Education* 60, no. 1 (2011): 115–144.

[11] Valerie Downs, Manoochehr Javidi, and Jon Nussbaum, "An Analysis of Teachers' Verbal Communication within the College Classroom: Use of Humor,

Self-Disclosure, and Narratives," *Communication Education* 37, no. 2 (1988): 127–140.

[12] Jennings Bryant, Paul Comisky, and Dolf Zillmann, "Teachers' Humor in the College Classroom," *Communication Education* 28, no. 2 (May 1979): 110–118.

[13] Bryant, Comisky, and Zillmann, "Teachers' Humor in the College Classroom."

[14] Bryant, Comisky, and Zillmann, "Teachers' Humor in the College Classroom."

[15] Lynn Barnett, "The Education of Playful Boys: Class Clowns in the Classroom," *Frontiers Psychology* 9, no. 232 (2018): 1–18, https://www.frontiersin.org/ articles/10.3389/fpsyg.2018.00232/full, 1.

[16] Barnett, "The Education of Playful Boys," 3.

[17] Barnett, "The Education of Playful Boys," 10–12.

[18] Barnett, "The Education of Playful Boys," 12.

[19] Barnett, "The Education of Playful Boys," 12.

[20] Barnett, "The Education of Playful Boys," 12–13.

[21] See *Association for Applied and Therapeutic Humor*, https://www.aath.org/ about-aath.

[22] Stuart Hellman, "Humor in the Classroom: STU'S Seven Simple Steps to Success," *College Teaching* 55, no.1 (2007): 37–39.

[23] Melanie Booth-Butterfield, Steven Booth-Butterfield, and Melissa Wanzer, "Funny Students Cope Better: Patterns of Humor Enactment and Coping Effectiveness," *Communication Quarterly* 55, no. 3 (2007): 299–315, https://doi.org/10.1080/01463370701490232.

[24] Booth-Butterfield, Booth-Butterfield, and Wanzer, "Funny Students Cope Better," 313.

[25] Tiffany Marie Freitas, "Students' Perception of Instructor Humor as a Predictor of Student Intellectual Stimulation, Academic Interest and Engagement," (master's thesis, University of the Pacific, 2018), https://scholarlycommons.pacific.edu/cgi/viewcontent.cgi?article=4116&context=uop_etds.

[26] Hellman, "Humor in the Classroom," 37.

[27] See J. A. Bryant's *Shakespeare and the Uses of Comedy* (Lexington, KY: University of Kentucky Press, 2014).

CHAPTER THREE:
On Joy—Unexpected Gifts of Delight

[1] C. S. Lewis, *The Screwtape Letters* (New York: Macmillan, 1968).

[2] C. S. Lewis, *Prayer: Letters to Malcolm* (Glasgow: Fontana, 1966), 93.

[3] Michael Ward, *Planet Narnia* (Oxford: Oxford University Press, 2010), 42.

[4] C. S. Lewis, *The Discarded Image* (Cambridge: Cambridge University Press, 1964), 117.

[5] Lewis, *The Discarded Image*, 117.

[6] C. S. Lewis, *That Hideous Strength* (1945; Samizdat, 2015), http://www.samizdat.qc.ca/arts/lit/PDFs/HideousStrength_CSL.pdf, 136.

[7] C. S. Lewis, *Studies in Medieval and Renaissance Literature* (Cambridge: Cambridge University Press, 1966), 131.

[8] C. S. Lewis, *Poems* (Orlando, FL: Harcourt Brace Jovanovich, 1964), 23; See Don King *C. S. Lewis, Poet: The Legacy of His Poetic Impulse* (Kent, OH: Kent State University, 2001), 172.

[9] Ward, *Planet Narnia*, 57.

[10] See Paul Ford, *Companion to Narnia* (New York: Harper and Row, 1980), 189.

[11] C. S. Lewis, *The Lion, the Witch, and the Wardrobe* (New York: Macmillan, 1950), 133.

[12] Lewis expounds: ". . . Nature in the form of air, water, food, etc., is *Bios*. The Spiritual life which is in God from all eternity, and which made the whole natural universe, is *Zoe*." C. S. Lewis, *Mere Christianity* (San Francisco, CA: Harper Collins, 2001), 159.

[13] Lewis, *The Lion, the Witch, and the Wardrobe*, 185.

[14] Lewis, *The Lion, the Witch, and the Wardrobe*, 185.

[15] C. S. Lewis, *Perelandra* (New York: Macmillan, 1965), 55.

[16] C. S. Lewis, *The Last Battle* (New York: Macmillan, 1956; Project Gutenberg, 2017), http://www.samizdat.qc.ca/arts/lit/PDFs/TheLastBattle_CSL.pdf , 98.

[17] Lewis, *The Last Battle*, 98.

[18] Lewis, *The Last Battle*, 111.

[19] G. K. Chesterton, "A Portrait," *The Wild Knight and Other Poems* (San Francisco: Ignatius Press, 1989).

[20] William Blake, "Auguries of Innocence," lines 55–62, Poetry Foundation, https://www.poetryfoundation.org/poems/43650/auguries-of-innocence.

[21] C. S. Lewis, *Essays Presented to Charles Williams* (Oxford: Oxford University Press, 1947), xii–xiii.

[22] Lewis, *Essays Presented to Charles Williams*, xii–xiii.

[23] See Maria Popova, "Trial, Triumph, and the Art of the Possible: The Remarkable Story Behind Beethoven's 'Ode to Joy,'" *The Marginalian*, https://www.themarginalian.org/2022/05/1 7/beethoven-ode-to-joy/.

[24] C. S. Lewis, *The Screwtape Letters*, (New York: Macmillan, 1968), xxxv.

[25] C. S. Lewis, *C. S. Lewis: Letters to Children*, eds. Lyle Dorsett and Marjorie Lamp Mead (New York: Macmillan, 1985), 89.

[26] G. K. Chesterton, *Tremendous Trifles* (London: Methuen, 1927), 200–1.

[27] Chesterton, *Tremendous Trifles*, 198.

[28] Aristotle, *On the Parts of Animals: Book III*, trans. William Ogle, https://penelope.uchicago.edu/aristotle/parts3.html, section 10.

[29] Donald O'Connor, "Make 'Em Laugh," Track 5 on *Singin' in the Rain* (Original Motion Picture Soundtrack), Turner Entertainment and Warner Bros. Entertainment, 1952.

[30] See "Molly Malone," *Wikipedia*, https://en.wikipedia.org/wiki/Molly_Malone.

[31] Charles Schulz, *Peanuts* (March 16, 1963), https://www.gocomics.com/peanuts/1963/03/16.

[32] Charles Dodgson, "Chapter X: The Lobster Quadrille," in *Alice's Adventures in Wonderland* (Project Gutenberg eBook, 2008), https://www.gutenberg.org/cache/epub/11/ pg11.txt.

CHAPTER FOUR:
On Fun—Unleashed Pleasures of Play

[1] See Anita Houck, "Thomas Aquinas Walks into a Bar: Vocation and (the Virtue of) Humor," *Network for Vocation in Undergraduate Education*, September 30, 2021,

https://vocationmatters.org/2021/09/30/vocation-and-the-virtue-of-humor/.

[2] C. S. Lewis, *The Screwtape Letters* (New York: Macmillan, 1968), 50; See also Jürgen Moltmann, *A Theology of Play* (New York: Harper and Row, 1972).

[3] Pieter Bruegel, *Kinderspiele*, 1560, oil on panel, 118 x 161 cm, Kunsthistorisches Museum Vienna, https://www.khm.at/de/object/321/.

[4] Desiderius Erasmus, "De utilitate Colloquiorum," *Collected Works of Erasmus*, 40, ed. Craig R. Thompson (Toronto, ON: University of Toronto Press, 1978), 1098.

[5] Edmund Spenser, *Spenser's The Faerie Queene, Book 1*, ed. George Armstrong Wauchope (New York: Macmillan, 1903).

[6] C. S. Lewis, *The Silver Chair* (New York: Macmillan, 1953), 204.

[7] Sophie K. Scott, Ceci Qing Cai, and Addison Billing, "Robert Provine: The Critical Human Importance of Laughter, Connections and Contagion," *Philosophical Transactions of the Royal Society B* 377, no. 1863 (September 21, 2022), https://doi.org/10.1098/rstb.2021.0178.

[8] Robert Provine, "Contagious Yawning and Laughing: Everyday Imitation- and Mirror-like Behavior," *Behavioral & Brain Science* 28, no. 2 (2005): 142.

[9] Fausto Caruana, Elisabetta Palagi, and Frans B. M. de Waal, "Cracking the Laugh Code: Laughter through the Lens of Biology, Psychology and Neuroscience," *Philosophical Transactions of the Royal Society B* 377, no. 1863 (November 7, 2022).

[10] Robert R. Provine, *Laughter: A Scientific Investigation* (New York: Penguin Books, 2000), 129.

[11] Daryl Austin, "Laughter really is contagious — and that's good," *The Washington Post*, January 15, 2023, https://www.washingtonpost.com/wellness/2023/01/15/laughing-is-contagious/.

[12] Eleni Loizou, "Humour: A different kind of play," *European Early Childhood Education Research Journal* 13, no. 2 (2005): 97–109.

[13] Loizou, "Humour: A different kind of play."

[14] Cited by John Kaag. "William James, Yoga, and the Secret of Happiness," *Wall Street Journal*, February 27, 2020, https://www.wsj.com/articles/william-james-yoga-and-the-secret-of-happiness-11582825877.

[15] See Rod Martin and Nicholas A. Kuiper, "Three Decades Investigating Humor and Laughter: An Interview with Professor Rod Martin," *Europe's Journal of Psychology* 12, no. 3 (2016): 498–512, http://doi.org/10.5964/ejop.v12i3.1119.

[16] Sandra Manninen, Lauri Tuominen, Robin I. Dunbar, et. al. "Social Laughter Triggers Endogenous Opioid Release in Humans," *Journal of Neuroscience* 37, no. 25 (June 2017): 6125–6131, http://doi.org/10.1523/JNEUROSCI.0688-16.2017.

[17] Manninen, Tuominen, Dunbar, et. al. "Social Laughter Triggers Endogenous Opioid Release in Humans," 6126.

[18] Sarah Algoe, "Gratitude and Shared Laughter are like Probiotics for your Relationship," *UNC College of Arts & Sciences*, November 13, 2023, https://college.unc.edu/2023/11/gratitude-algoe/.

[19] C. S. Lewis, *The Voyage of the Dawn Treader* (London, 1964; Project Gutenberg, 2017), www.samizdat.qc.ca/arts/lit/PDFs/VoyageoftheDawnTreader_CSL.pdf, 93.

[20] James Sully, *An Essay in Laughter: Its Forms, Its Causes, Its Development and Its Value* (London: Longmans, Green, and Company, 1902), 237.

[21] Sully, *An Essay in Laughter*, 237.

[22] G. K. Chesterton, "W. W. Jacobs," in *A Handful of Authors*, ed. Dorothy Collins (New York: Sheed and Ward, 1953).

[23] Chesterton, "W. W. Jacobs," in *A Handful of Authors*.

[24] Lewis, *The Voyage of the Dawn Treader*, 90.

[25] Lewis, *The Voyage of the Dawn Treader*, 91.

[26] Lewis, *The Voyage of the Dawn Treader*, 91.

[27] Lewis, *The Voyage of the Dawn Treader*, 91.

[28] Lewis, *The Voyage of the Dawn Treader*, 92.

[29] Lewis, *The Voyage of the Dawn Treader*, 93.

[30] "Dead Parrot Sketch" series 1, episode 8 "Full Frontal Nudity," *Monty Python's Flying Circus*, written by Eric Idle and performed by Eric Idle and Terry Jones. Aired October 19, 1969, BBC.

[31] "Nudge, Nudge sketch," series 1, episode 3, "How to Recognise Different Types of Trees From Quite a Long Way Away," *Monty Python's Flying Circus*, written by John Cleese and Graham Chapman and performed by John Cleese and Michael Palin. Aired December 7, 1969, BBC.

[32] Lewis, *Voyage of the Dawn Treader*, 74.

[33] Lewis, *Voyage of the Dawn Treader*, 76.

[34] Lewis, *Voyage of the Dawn Treader*, 76.

[35] John Fisher, *What a Performance: the Life of Sid Field* (London: Seeley, 1975).

[36] Fisher, *What a Performance*; See also *The Goon Show*, aired May 28, 1951, BBC, https://www.bbc.com/historyofthebbc/anniversaries/may/the-goon-show.

[37] Lewis, *Voyage of the Dawn Treader*, 77.

[38] Lewis, *Voyage of the Dawn Treader*, 79–80.

[39] Lewis, *Voyage of the Dawn Treader*, 94.

[40] C. S. Lewis, *Prince Caspian* (London: Geoffrey Bles, 1964; Project Gutenberg, 2017), http://www.samizdat.qc.ca/arts/lit/PDFs/PrinceCaspian_CSL.pdf , 84.

[41] Aristotle, *Nicomachean Ethics*, trans. H. Rackham, Loeb Classical Library 73 (Cambridge, MA: Harvard University Press, 1994), IV: 8.

[42] Aristotle, *Nicomachean Ethics*, IV: 8.

[43] Aristotle, *Nicomachean Ethics*, IV: 8.

[44] Cited in Michael Screech, *Laughter at the Foot of the Cross* (Chicago, IL: University of Chicago Press, 2015), 138.

[45] C. S. Lewis, *The Lion, the Witch, and the Wardrobe* (New York: Macmillan, 1950).

[46] Cited in John Morreall *Taking Laughter Seriously* (Albany: State University of New York, 1963), 16. For Kant, laughter is "an affection arising from the sudden transformation of a strained expectation into nothing," a version of both the relief and incongruity theories (16).

[47] G. K. Chesterton, *Orthodoxy* (Toronto, ON: Doubleday, 1956), 60.

[48] Chesterton, *Orthodoxy*, 60.

[49] Geva Skard and Anita C. Bundy, *Test of Playfulness*, 1–23, https://www.chiro-credit.com/downloads/pediatrics/pediatrics215.pdf

[50] Skard and Bundy, *Test of Playfulness*, 2.

[51] Skard and Bundy, *Test of Playfulness*, 3.

[52] Skard and Bundy, *Test of Playfulness*, 3.

[53] Skard and Bundy, *Test of Playfulness*, 3.

[54] Skard and Bundy, *Test of Playfulness*, 6.

[55] Eunjoo Jung and Bora Jin, "College Coursework on Children's Play and Future Early Childhood Educators' Intended Practices: The Mediating Influence of Perceptions

of Play," *Early Childhood Education Journal* 43 (2015): 299–306.

[56] Jung and Jin, "College Coursework on Children's Play and Future Early Childhood Educators' Intended Practices".

[57] Elizabeth Jones and Gretchen Reynolds, *The Play's the Thing: Teachers' Roles in Children's Play* (New York: Teachers College Press, 2011).

[58] Jeffrey Trawick-Smith and Tracy Dziurgot, "Untangling Teacher–child Play Interactions: Do Teacher Education and Experience Influence 'Good-Fit' Responses to Children's Play?" *Journal of Early Childhood Teacher Education* 31, no. 2 (2010): 106–128.

[59] Trawick-Smith and Dziurgot, "Untangling Teacher–child Play Interactions."

[60] Sheila Kenninson, *The Cognitive Neuroscience of Humor* (American Psychological Association, 2020).

[61] *Inside Out*, directed by Pete Docter and Ronnie Del Carmen (Burbank, CA: Pixar Animation Studios, 2015).

[62] Eva Froehlich, Apoorva Rajiv Madipakkam, Barbara Craffonara, Christina Bolte, Anne-Katrin Muth, and Soyoung Q. Park, "A short humorous intervention protects against subsequent psychological stress and attenuates cortisol levels without affecting attention," *Scientific Reports* 11, no.7284 (2021): 1–9, https://doi.org/10.1038/s41598-021-86527-1

[63] Rod Martin, "Humor, Laughter, and Physical Health: Methodological Issues and Research Findings" *Psychological Bulletins* 4 (July 2001): 504–19.

[64] Lee S. Berk, "Mind, Body, Spirit: Exploring the Mind, Body, Spirit Connection Through Research On Mirthful Laughter," in *Spirituality, Health, and Wholeness: An Introductory Guide for Health Care Professionals*, eds. Siroj Sorajjakool and Henry Lamberton (Binghamton, NY: Haworth, 2004).

[65] Asking "Do Children Laugh Much More Often than Adults Do?" Rod Martin raises the possibility that the differences are not that great, with the presence of social interaction augmenting all ages of laughter. Kristina Klinker, "Who laughs more often, children or adults?" *Journal of Unsolved Questions*, November 11, 2014, https://junq.info/?p=2427.

[66] Delthia Ricks, "Laughter: Best Medicine," *Virginian-Pilot*, February 17, 1997, E9.

[67] Ricks, "Laughter: Best Medicine."

[68] Norman Cousins, *Anatomy of an Illness* (New York: Norton, 2005).

[69] John Morreall, *Laughing all the Way: Your Sense of Humor Don't Leave Home without It* (Melbourne, FL: Motivational, 2016), 181. For example, one jest went: "Today in Germany the proper form of grace is 'Thank God and Hitler.' 'But suppose the Führer dies?' 'Then you just thank God.'"

[70] Cal Samra, *The Joyful Christ: The Healing Power of Humor* (San Francisco: Harper & Row, 1986), 35.

[71] Cited in Alzina Stone Dale, *Outline of Sanity: A Life of G. K. Chesterton* (Grand Rapids, MI: Eerdmans, 1982), 113.

[72] As Dante comes to the highest celestial sphere, he halts hearing a sound that he'd never heard before:"*Me sembiana un riso del universe*," which translated means it sounded "like the laughter of the universe"(*Paradisio* XXVII: 1–5).

[73] As cited in David Savage, "Expressions Trigger Emotions: Putting on a Happy Face: It Works Researcher Says," *Los Angeles Times*, May 29, 1985, https://www.latimes.com/archives/la-xpm-1985-05-29-mn-7418-story.html

[74] John Morreall, *Comic Relief* (Hoboken, NJ: Wiley-Blackwell, 2009), 2.

[75] Paul Ekman, *Unmasking the Face: A Guide to Recognizing Emotions from Facial Expressions* (Cambridge, MA: Malor, 2003).

[76] While Fritz Strack could not replicate his research on the "Sad Face" experiment, it is still fun to try out. See Daniel Engber, "Sad Face," *Slate*, August 28, 2016, https://www.slate.com/articles/health_and_science/cover_story/2016/08/can_smiling_make_you_happier_maybe_maybe_not_we_have_no_idea.html.

[77] See "Duchenne Machine –1850," *The National MagLab*, https://nationalmaglab.org/magnet-academy/history-of-electricity-magnetism/museum/duchenne-machine-1850/.

[78] Michael Dufner, Martin Brümmer, Joanne M. Chung, et al., "Does Smile Intensity in Photographs Really Predict Longevity? A Replication and Extension of Abel and Kruger (2010)" *Psychological Science* 29, no. 1 (January 29, 2018): 147–153, https://doi.org/10.1177/0956797617734315, 642.

[79] Leo Widrich, "The Science of Smiling: A Guide to the World's Most Powerful Gesture," *Buffer*, April 9, 2013, https://buffer.com/resources/the-science-of-smiling-a-guide-to-humans-most-powerful-gesture/.

[80] Widrich, "The Science of Smiling."

[81] Dr. Hagerstaff, "The Zygomatic Exercise." This quotation was taken from a speech given sometime in the 1980s at a forgotten location, recorded on audiotape and then scribbled on a yellow piece of paper that was serendipitously discovered in an old book.

[82] See Christian F. Hempelmann, "The Laughter of the 1962 Tanganyika 'laughter epidemic,'" *International Journal of Humor Research* 20, no. 1 (2007): 49–71, http://doi.org/10.1515/HUMOR.2007.003.

[83] See James A. Beverly, *Holy Laughter and the Toronto Blessing: An Investigative Report* (Grand Rapids: Zondervan, 1995).

[84] Cited in Terry Lindvall, "Toward a Divine Comedy: A Plagiarized History, Theology and Physiology of Christian Faith and Laughter," *The Lamp-Post of the Southern California C. S. Lewis Society* 27, no. 3 (Fall 2003): 12–31, https://www.jstor.org/stable/45347475.

[85] Latin meaning "a sweet and useful thing," here suggesting that education should be both "pleasurable and profitable"; See "dulce et utile," *Latin is Simple*, https://www.latin-is-simple.com/en/vocabulary/phrase/507/.

CHAPTER FIVE:
Joke Proper—Ingenuity of Wit and Jests

[1] C. S. Lewis, *C. S. Lewis: Letters to Children*, eds. Lyle Dorsett and Marjorie Lamp Mead (New York: Macmillan, 1985), 28.

[2] Lewis, *C. S. Lewis: Letters to Children*, 57.

[3] Jaak Panksepp and Jeff Burgdorf, "'Laughing' Rats and the Evolutionary Antecedents of Human Joy?" *Physiological Behavior* 79, no. 3 (2003): 533–47, Abstract, https://doi.org/10.1016/S0031-9384(03)00159-8.

[4] Panksepp and Burgdorf, "'Laughing' Rats and the Evolutionary Antecedents of Human Joy?" Abstract.

[5] John Morreall, *Taking Laughter Seriously* (Albany, NY: State University of New York, 1983), 6.

⁶ See Terry Lindvall, "The Fun in Nature," *Surprised by Laughter* (Nashville, TN: Thomas Nelson, 1996), 159–170.

⁷ C. S. Lewis, *The Magician's Nephew* (New York, 1966; Project Gutenberg, 2017), 71, http://www.samizdat.qc.ca/arts/lit/PDFs/MagiciansNephew_CSL.pdf; in a letter to his friend Arthur Greeves, Lewis wrote about an old jackdaw that he called Jack, perhaps revealing his personal connection to this loud, socially clumsy, and joking creature.

⁸ Lewis, *The Magician's Nephew*, 71.

⁹ Lewis, *The Magician's Nephew*, 71.

¹⁰ Lewis, *C. S. Lewis: Letters to Children*, 47.

¹¹ C. S. Lewis, *The Lion, the Witch, and the Wardrobe* (New York: Macmillan, 1950), 9. Lewis borrowed merrily from Edith Nesbitt's children's story, *The Aunt and Amabel* (1912) for these silly terms.

¹² See Ann S. Masten, "Humor and Competence in School-aged Children," *Child Development* 57, no. 2 (1986).

¹³ See Nel Warnars-Kleverlaan, Louis Oppenheimer, and Larry Sherman, "To Be or Not to Be Humorous: Does It make a Difference?" *Humor* 9, no. 2 (1996).

¹⁴ Patti Valkenburg and Jessica Taylor Piotrowski, *Plugged In* (New Haven, CT: Yale University Press, 2017), 84.

¹⁵ C. S. Lewis, *The Silver Chair* (London, 1965; Project Gutenberg, 2017), 20, http://www.samizdat.qc.ca/arts/lit/PDFs/TheSilverChair_CSL.pdf.

¹⁶ Lewis, *The Silver Chair*, 21.

¹⁷ Lewis, *The Silver Chair*, 29.

¹⁸ Lewis, *The Silver Chair*, 29–30.

¹⁹ Roger von Oech, *A Whack on the Side of the Head: How You Can Be More Creative*, Third edition (New York: Warner, 1998).

²⁰ von Oech, *A Whack on the Side of the Head*, 28.

²¹ C. S. Lewis, *Surprised by Joy* (Orlando, FL: Harcourt Brace Jovanovich, 1955), 14–15.

²² Jared Lobdell, *Eight Children in Narnia: The Making of a Children's Story* (Chicago, IL: Open Court, 2016).

²³ Lewis, *C. S. Lewis: Letters to Children*, 14.

²⁴ Lobdell, *Eight Children in Narnia*, 44.

²⁵ See John Tenniel, "The Ass in the Lion's Skin," 1848, wood engraving, 17.5 x 12 cm, *New York Public Library Digital Collections*, accessed August 21, 2024, https://digitalcollections.nypl.org/items/6945c588-7bfa-311f-e040-e00a180608ea.

²⁶ Hilaire Belloc, *Cautionary Tales for Children* (London: Duckworth, 1957; Project Gutenberg, 2008), https://www.gutenberg.org/files/27424/27424-h/27424-h.htm.

²⁷ Heinrich Hoffman, *Struwwelpeter: Merry Tales and Funny Pictures* (New York: Frederick Warne & Co.; Project Gutenberg, 2004), https://www.gutenberg.org/files/12116/12116-h/12116-h.htm.

²⁸ See "Caption Contest Rules," *New Yorker Magazine*, https://www.newyorker.com/about/caption-contest-rules.

²⁹ Marc Aguert, Coralie le Vallois, Karine Martel, and Virginie Laval, "'That's really Clever!' Ironic Hyperbole Understanding in Children," *Journal of Children Language* 45, no. 1 (2018), 260–272.

³⁰ Lewis, *The Silver Chair*, chap. 9: 67–74.

[31] *The Twilight Zone*, season 3, episode 24, "To Serve Man," directed by Richard L. Bare, written by Rod Sterling, aired March 2, 1962, on CBS.

[32] Lewis, *The Silver Chair*, 59.

[33] Lewis, *The Silver Chair*, 57–58.

[34] Lewis, *The Silver Chair*, 58.

[35] Lewis, *The Silver Chair*, 65.

[36] Lewis, *The Silver Chair*, 62.

[37] Lewis, *The Silver Chair*, 61.

[38] Lewis, *The Silver Chair*, 66.

[39] C. S. Lewis, *Voyage of the Dawn Treader* (New York: Macmillan, 1952), 1.

[40] Lewis, *Voyage of the Dawn Treader*, 5.

[41] Lewis, *The Magician's Nephew*, 74.

[42] Lewis, *The Magician's Nephew*, 75.

[43] Lewis, *The Magician's Nephew*, 75.

[44] Lewis, *The Magician's Nephew*, 78.

[45] Lewis, *The Magician's Nephew*, 78.

[46] C. S. Lewis, *The Horse and His Boy* (New York: Macmillan, 1954), 209

[47] Lewis, *The Horse and His Boy*, 234.

[48] Lewis, *The Horse and His Boy*, 211.

[49] Lewis, *The Horse and His Boy*, 235.

[50] Lewis, *The Horse and His Boy*, 219.

[51] Lewis, *The Horse and His Boy*, 221.

[52] King Lune laughs at the "taunt of a pajock." However, he also reprimands his own son Corin for unseemly mocking. When Rabadash continues to prate and prattle, trying to frighten his conquerors, he warns, "Beware! The bolt of Tash falls from above!" Corin retorts, "does it ever get caught on a hook half way?" While such a rejoinder elicits laughter, the good-hearted King Lune reins in his son, teaching him that one should "Never taunt a man save when he is strong than you; then, as you please." There is, for Lewis, an ethic for humor. One should save one's satire for those who are more powerful. As Lewis said elsewhere, he would rather step on the toe of a live giant than cut off the head of a dead one, and while more dangerous, it is also more fun.

[53] James Sully, *An Essay in Laughter: Its Forms, Its Causes, Its Development and Its Value* (London: Longmans, Green, and Company, 1902), 245.

[54] Sully, *An Essay in Laughter*, 245.

[55] Sully, *An Essay in Laughter*, 267.

[56] "Long live the differences (as between the sexes)." *Merriam-Webster*, "Vive la difference," accessed August 19, 2024, https://www.merriam-webster.com/dictionary/vive%20la%20différence.

[57] Lewis found George Meredith's comic spirit to be lacking. True comedy for the Egoist was that it would awaken "thoughtful laughter." However, such a Manichean or gnostic worldview delighted only the mind, and not the heart and belly as well. See Lindvall, *Surprised by Laughter*, 213.

[58] C. S. Lewis, *Prince Caspian* (London: Geoffrey Bles, 1964; Project Gutenberg, 2017), http://www.samizdat.qc.ca/arts/lit/PDFs/PrinceCaspian_CSL.pdf, 63.

[59] See "Taba Model," *Academically and Intellectually Gifted Handbook for Teachers*, https://macsaigteacher.weebly.com/taba-model.html#:~:text=Hilda%20Taba%20is%20the%20developer,in%20the%20article%20of%20%22change%22.

[60] Lewis, *The Voyage of the Dawn Treader*, 202–203.

[61] Lewis *The Voyage of the Dawn Treader*, 174, 188.

[62] G. K. Chesterton, *All Things Considered* (Chester Springs, PA: Dufour, 1969), 14.

[63] One of the primary concerns is with definition. A translation of Freud's *Witz* connotes more than "wit" and spills into the category of jokes. Lewis, on the other hand, devoted an entire chapter on the linguistic evolution of the word "Wit" (with *Ingenium*) from mind, intelligence, and good sense to its "dangerous sense" of being clever repartee. See *Studies in Words* (Cambridge: Cambridge University Press, 1967), 86–110. Allegedly, one reason Freud felt compelled to investigate this phenomenon of joking was that a reader of *The Interpretation of Dreams* protested that the dreams were replete with what appeared to be puns and jokes. ("Ah," said the Episcopal priest, "I dreamed that the steeple of my cathedral fell off this morning. What can it mean?") Like Lenny Bruce, Freud compiled his collection of Jewish anecdotes both as data and as personal security. Sigmund Freud, *Jokes and Their Relation to the Unconscious*, ed. and trans. James Strachey (New York: Norton, 1960), 103.

[64] Freud, *Jokes and Their Relation to the Unconscious*, 103.

[65] Freud, *Jokes and Their Relation to the Unconscious*.

[66] Freud, *Jokes and Their Relation to the Unconscious*, 105.

[67] Freud, *Jokes and Their Relation to the Unconscious*, 88.

[68] Thomas Hobbes, *Leviathan* (1651; Project Gutenberg, 2002), bk. 1, chap. 13, https://www.gutenberg.org/files/3207/3207-h/3207-h.htm#link2H_4_0117.

[69] See "Humor," *Internet Encyclopedia of Philosophy*, https://iep.utm.edu/humor/.

[70] C. S. Lewis, *Miracles* (New York: Macmillan, 1947), 132.

[71] C. S. Lewis, *The Screwtape Letters* (New York: Macmillan, 1968), 50.

[72] C. S. Lewis, *The Four Loves* (Orlando, FL: Harcout Brace Jovanovich, 1960), 143.

[73] Lewis, *The Four Loves*, 179.

[74] William Griffin, *Clive Staples Lewis: A Dramatic Life* (New York: Harper and Row, 1986), 430.

[75] This line has also been famously said by German organist and composer, Max Reger, regarding a critic's review. It is originally attributed to Voltaire.

[76] Cited in Lindvall, *Surprised by Laughter*, 277, 284.

[77] Robert Provine, *Laughter: A Scientific Study* (New York: Penguin, 2000), 41.

[78] Provine, *Laughter*, 41.

[79] Teri Evans-Palmer, *The Art of Teaching with Humor* (Lausanne, Switzerland: Peter Lang, 2021), 15.

[80] Rod A. Martin and Thomas Ford, *The Psychology of Humor: An Integrative Approach* (London: Academic, 2018).

[81] Roni Natov and Geraldine DeLuca, "An Interview with Arnold Lobel," *The Lion and the Unicorn* 1, no. 1 (1977): 72–96, 84.

[82] See Michael Cart, *What's So Funny? Wit and Humor in Children's Literature* (New York: HarperCollins, 1995), 89–9; Arnold Lobel, *Frog and Toad are Friends* (HarperCollins, 2011).

[83] Milika Andrews – ESPN, "Don't bet against the fat boy! – Nikola Jokic on winning NBA Finals MVP & his appetite to win more," June 13, 2023, YouTube video, 3:23, https://www.youtube.com/watch?v=HSjbDYjtWck

[84] Rod A. Martin, *Test Your Human Style: Humors Style Questionnaire*, http://www.humorstyles.com.

[85] See Martin, *Test Your Human Style*.

[86] Cheryl Mizerny, "Six Reasons Why Middle School Rocks," *Middle Web*, September 6, 2015, https://www.middleweb.com/24949/six-reasons-why-middle-school-rocks/.
[87] Lewis, *Screwtape Letters*, 52.

CHAPTER SIX:
On Flippancy—Descent into Darkness

[1] Cited in Terry Lindvall, *Surprised by Laughter* (Nashville, TN: Thomas Nelson, 1996), 379.
[2] G. K. Chesterton, *Father Brown Omnibus* (New York: Dodd, Mead & Co., 1982), 758.
[3] C. S. Lewis, *Surprised by Joy* (Orlando, FL: Harcourt Brace Jovanovich, 1955), 106.
[4] C. S. Lewis, *The Lion, the Witch, and the Wardrobe* (New York: Macmillan, 1950; Project Gutenberg, 2017), 16, http://www.samizdat.qc.ca/arts/lit/PDFs/LionWitch-Wardrobe_CSL.pdf.
[5] Lewis, *The Lion, the Witch, and the Wardrobe*, 17.
[6] Lewis, *The Lion, the Witch, and the Wardrobe*, 59.
[7] G. K. Chesterton, *The Common Man* (New York: Sheed & Ward, 1950), 157–159.
[8] Chesterton, *The Common Man*, 158.
[9] G. K. Chesterton, *A Handful of Authors* (New York: Sheed & Ward, 1953), 28–29.
[10] Lewis, *The Lion, the Witch, and the Wardrobe*, 31.
[11] Lewis, *The Lion, the Witch, and the Wardrobe*, 19.
[12] Lewis, *The Lion, the Witch, and the Wardrobe*, 52.
[13] John H. Hoover and Glenn Olson, "Sticks and Stones May Break Their Bones: Teasing as Bullying," *Reclaiming Children and Youth* 9, no. 2 (Summer 2000): 87.
[14] Lewis, *The Lion, the Witch, and the Wardrobe*, 22–23.
[15] Lewis, *The Lion, the Witch, and the Wardrobe*, 50.
[16] Michael A. Screech, *Laughter at the Foot of the Cross* (Chicago: University of Chicago Press, 1997).
[17] Lewis, *The Lion, the Witch, and the Wardrobe*, 81.
[18] Fra Angelico, *Mocking of Christ*, 1440–42, fresco, 181 cm x 151 cm, Florence, Museum of San Marco; Hieronymus Bosch, *Christ Carrying the Cross*, c. 1510, oil on panel, 83.5 x 76.7 cm, Belgium, Museum of Fine Arts; Lucas Cranach the Elder, *The Mocking of Christ*, 1472–1553, oil on panel, 35.9 x 28 cm, France, private collection.
[19] Lewis, *The Lion, the Witch, and the Wardrobe*, 81.
[20] Rene T. Proyer, Lukas E. Meier, Tracey Platt, and Willibald Ruch, "Dealing with Laughter and Ridicule in Adolescence: Relations with Bullying and Emotional Responses," *Social Psychology of Education* 16 (2013): 399–420; Tracey Platt, "Emotional Responses to Ridicule and Teasing: Should Gelotophobes React Differently?" *Humor: International Journal of Humor Research* 21 (2008): 105–128.
[21] Stephanie V. Klages and James H. Wirth, "Excluded by Laughter: Laughing Until it Hurts Someone Else," *The Journal of Social Psychology* 154, no. 1 (2014): 8–13.
[22] See Rod A. Martin, Patricia Puhlik-Doris, Gwen Larsen, Jeanette Gray, and Kelly Weir, "Individual differences in uses of humor and their relation to psychological well-being: Development of the Humor Styles Questionnaire," *Journal of Research in Personality* 37, no. 1 (2003): 48–75, https://doi.org/10.1016/S0092-6566(02)00534-2.
[23] C. S. Lewis, *The Screwtape Letters* (New York: Macmillan, 1968; Project

Gutenberg, 2016), http://www.samizdat.qc.ca/arts/lit/PDFs/ScrewtapeLetters_CSL.pdf, 22.

[24] Lewis, *The Screwtape Letters*, 22.

[25] C. S. Lewis, *The Last Battle* (New York: HarperCollins, 1984), 139.

[26] G. K. Chesterton, *As I Was Saying* (Grand Rapids, MI: Eerdmans, 1985), 266.

[27] Lewis, *The Last Battle*, 139.

[28] Lewis, *The Last Battle*, 71, 148.

[29] Lewis, *The Screwtape Letters*, 22.

[30] Mark Twain, *Following the Equator* (Hartford, CT: 1898; Project Gutenberg, 2006), https://gutenberg.org/files/2895/2895-h/2895-h.htm.

[31] Claire Fox, S. C. Hunter, and S. E. Jones, "The Relationship between Peer Victimization and Children's Humor Styles: It's No Laughing Matter!" *Social Development* 24, no. 3 (2014): 443–461.

[32] John Morreall, *Comic Relief* (Hoboken, NJ: Wiley-Blackwell, 2009), xii.

[33] See Erin Wais, "Trained Incapacity: Thorstein Veblen and Kenneth Burke," *The Journal of the Kenneth Burke Society* 2, no. 1 (Fall 2005), https://www.kbjournal.org/wais.

[34] Henri Bergson, *Laughter: An Essay on the Meaning of the Comic*, trans. Cloudesley Brereton and Fred Rothwell (1900; Project Gutenberg, 2003), https://www.gutenberg.org/cache/epub/4352/pg4352.txt.

[35] Ken Kesey, *One Flew Over the Cuckoo's Nest* (New York: Signet, 1962), 41.

[36] See Neil Postman, *Amusing Ourselves to Death: Public Discourse in the Age of Show Business* (New York: Penguin, 1985).

[37] H. Allen Smith, "Humorist," *Psychology Today*, August 1983, cited in "The Role of Laughter in the Christian Life," *C. S. Lewis Institute*, March 18, 2015, https://www.cslewisinstitute.org/resources/the-role-of-laughter-in-the-christian-life/.

[38] William Hazlitt, *Lectures on the English Comic Writers* (London: J. Templeman, 1841), https://www.loc.gov/item/15008270/.

[39] C. S. Lewis, *The World's Last Night* (Orlando, FL: Harcourt Brace Jovanovich, 1959), 48.

[40] Jan Steen, *As the Old Sing, So Pipe the Young*, c. 1668–1670, oil on canvas, 133.7 x 162.5 cm, Netherlands, Mauritshuis.

[41] Barbara Mikkelson, "Lipstick on Bathroom Mirror," *Snopes*, March 17, 2001, https://www.snopes.com/fact-check/the-little-print-cesses/.

[42] C. S. Lewis, *Experiment in Criticism* (Cambridge: Cambridge University Press, 1961), 112.

CHAPTER SEVEN:
Tricks of the Trade

[1] C. S. Lewis, *The Abolition of Man* (New York: Macmillan, 1965), 13.

[2] Lewis, *The Abolition of Man*, 13.

[3] See John A. Banas, Norah Dunbar, Dariela Rodriguez, and Shr-Jie Liu, "A Review of Humor in Educational Settings: Four Decades of Research," *Communication Education* 60, no. 1 (2011): 115–144, https://doi.org/10.1080/03634523.2010.496867.

[4] Student Researcher Virginia Wesleyan University (Fall 2019).

[5] Leo Widrich, "The Science of Smiling: What Happens to our Brain

When We Smile," *LinkedIn*, October 18, 2016, https://www.linkedin.com/pulse/smile-kate-bickford.

⁶ "Saint of the Month: Heaven's Heroes—Saint Mother Teresa of Kolkata," *Missionary Childhood*, September 2020, https://www.propfaithboston.org/documents/52746/2473729/Saint+Mother+Teresa.pdf/4098f8fe-a287-abf5-ba5c-83e4de779e63.

⁷ Joel Chandler Harris, "Brother Rabbit's Laughing-Place," in *Told by Uncle Remus: New Stories of the Old Plantation* (New York: Grosset & Dunlap, 1903), *SurLaLune Fairy Tales*, https://www.surlalunefairytales.com/book.php?id=117&tale=4956.

⁸ Shulamit Pinchover, "The Relation between Teachers' and Children's Playfulness: A Pilot Study," *Frontiers in Psychology* 8 (2017), https://doi.org/10.3389/fpsyg.2017.02214.

⁹ Sandra Manninen, Lauri Tuominen, Robin I. Dunbar, et al., "Social Laughter Triggers Endogenous Opioid Release in Humans," *Journal of Neuroscience* 37, no. 25 (2017): 6125–6131, https://doi.org/10.1523/JNEUROSCI.0688-16.2017.

¹⁰ Herman Melville, *Moby Dick; Or, The Whale* (1851; Project Gutenberg, 2001) https://www.gutenberg.org/cache/epub/2701/pg2701.txt.

¹¹ *Beowulf*, trans. Lesslie Hall (Boston: D. C. Heath & Co, 1892), https://tile.loc.gov/storage-services/public/gdcmassbookdig/beowulfanglosaxo00hall/ beowulfanglosaxo00hall.pdf.

¹² Charles Dickens, *A Christmas Carol* (Philadelphia, PA: J. B. Lippincott Co., 1915; Project Gutenberg, 2007), https://www.gutenberg.org/cache/epub/24022/pg24022-images.html, 97.

¹³ Dickens, *A Christmas Carol*, 147.

¹⁴ Mark Twain, *The Adventures of Tom Sawyer* (Hartford, CT: The American Publishing Co., 1884; Project Gutenberg, 2004), https://www.gutenberg.org/cache/epub/74/pg74-images.html, 12.

¹⁵ Homer, *The Odyssey*, ed. Robert Squillace, trans. George Herbert Palmer (New York: Barnes & Noble Classics, 2003), 111.

¹⁶ Homer, *The Odyssey*, 112.

¹⁷ G. K. Chesterton, "On Humour," *Encyclopedia Britannica*, 14th edition (New York: Enclyclopedia Britannica Inc., 1929), 883–885.

¹⁸ C. S. Lewis, *A Grief Observed* (Minneapolis, MN: Seabury, 1961), 57.

¹⁹ See Alleen Pace Nilsen and Don L. F. Nilsen, *Names and Naming in Young Adult Literature* (Lanham, MD: Scarecrow, 2007).

²⁰ Alleen Pace Nilsen and Don L. F. Nilsen, *The Language of Humor* (Cambridge: Cambridge University Press, 2018).

CONCLUSION

¹ Walt Whitman, "There was a child went forth every day," 1855, *Poets.org*, https://poets.org/poem/there-was-child-went-forth-every-day.

² Johann Wolfgang von Goethe cited in Terry Lindvall, *Surprised by Laughter* (Nashville, TN: Thomas Nelson, 1996), 23.

³ James Sully, *An Essay in Laughter: Its Forms, Its Causes, Its Development and Its Value* (London: Longmans, Green, and Company, 1902), 426.

⁴ G. K. Chesterton, *The Common Man* (New York: Sheed & Ward, 1950), 158.

"The secret of life lies in laughter and humility." G. K. Chesterton, *Heretics* (San Francisco, CA: Ignatius, 1986). One line from William Makepeace Thackeray's "A Grumble about the Christmas Books," *Fraser's Magazine* (January 1847) sums it up: "Love is the humorists' best characteristic, and gives that charming ring to their laughter in which all the good-natured world joins in chorus" (123).

[5] C. S. Lewis, *Mere Christianity* (San Francisco, CA: HarperCollins, 2001), 198–199.

[6] Lewis, *Mere Christianity*, 199.

[7] Lewis, *Mere Christianity*, 199.

[8] C. S. Lewis, *The Abolition of Man* (New York: Macmillan, 1965), 23.

[9] C. S. Lewis, *The Last Battle* (New York: Macmillan, 1956), 170.

[10] Desiderius Erasmus, *In Praise of Folly* (London: Reeves and Turner, 1876; Project Gutenberg, 2009), https://www.gutenberg.org/files/30201/30201-h/30201-h.htm.

[11] Charles Dodgson, *Alice's Adventures in Wonderland*, Millenium Fulcrum Edition (Project Gutenberg, 2008), https://www.gutenberg.org/cache/epub/11/pg11.txt, 2.

Index

About the Authors

Terry Lindvall (Ph.D. University of Southern California) occupies the C. S. Lewis Chair of Communication and Christian Thought at Virginia Wesleyan University. He has taught on Communication, Theology, and Laughter (and Film) at Duke University Divinity School, Regent University, and was the Mason Fellow at the College of William and Mary. He has published fourteen books including award-winning *Sanctuary Cinema* (NYU Press, 2007), *God Mocks* (NYU Press, 2015), *Divine Film Comedies* (Routledge, 2016), and *Animated Parables* (Lexington Press, 2023). He just produced the documentary feature film, Hollywood, *Teach us to Pray* (2023), based on his book, *God on the Big Screen* (NYU Press, 2019). He once pretended for over four years to be a University President at Regent University.

Cary Joseph (BA in English, James Madison University; MAT, James Madison University) has taught 7th grade English for seven years and now teaches at Old Donation Gifted School in Virginia Beach, Virginia. His wife, **Caroline Joseph** (BA in English, James Madison University, MAT, University of Virginia) taught 8th grade English for five years. She is the author of the children's book, *The Girl Who Couldn't Laugh*. They met in college when Cary noticed her license plate ERASMUS and quoted the Dutch educator to her. They have one very precocious and ebullient child, Joy, who at 6 months knew what those words meant.